# Company's Coming ®

# Perfect Pasta
# And Sauces

*Jean Paré*

**www.companyscoming.com**
visit our website

## Front Cover

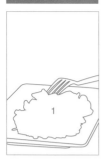

1. Smoky Chicken Penne,
   page 65

Props courtesy of: Danesco Inc.

## Back Cover

1. Sweet Potato And Kale
   Penne, page 138
2. Aniseed Tomato Fusilli,
   page 145

Props courtesy of: Cherison Enterprises
Inc.

*We gratefully acknowledge the following suppliers for their generous support of our Test and Photography Kitchens:*

Broil King Barbecues          Hamilton Beach® Canada          Proctor Silex® Canada
Corelle®                      Lagostina®                      Tupperware®

**Perfect Pasta And Sauces**

First Printing August 2008

**Library and Archives Canada Cataloguing in Publication**
Paré, Jean, date
Perfect pasta and sauces / Jean Paré.
(Original series)
Includes index.
ISBN 978-1-897069-63-9
1. Cookery (Pasta). 2. Sauces. I. Title. II. Series: Paré, Jean,
date- . Original series.
TX809.M17P373 2008          641.8'22          C2008-901312-3

Published by
**Company's Coming Publishing Limited**
2311 – 96 Street
Edmonton, Alberta, Canada T6N 1G3
Tel: 780-450-6223   Fax: 780-450-1857
www.companyscoming.com

Company's Coming is a registered trademark owned by
Company's Coming Publishing Limited

We acknowledge the financial support of the Government of Canada through the Book Publishing Industry Development Program (BPIDP) for our publishing activities.

Printed in China

# Need more recipes?

Six *"sneak preview"* recipes are featured online **with every new book released.**

Visit us at ➘
*www.companyscoming.com*

# Company's Coming Cookbooks

## Original Series

- Softcover, 160 pages
- 6" x 9" (15 cm x 23 cm) format
- Lay-flat plastic comb binding
- Full-colour photos
- Nutrition information

Quick & easy recipes! Everyday ingredients!

## Lifestyle Series

- Softcover, 160 pages
- 8" x 10" (20 cm x 25 cm) format
- Paperback
- Full-colour photos
- Nutrition information

## Most Loved Recipe Collection

- Hardcover, 128 pages
- 8 3/4" x 8 3/4" (22 cm x 22 cm) format
- Durable sewn binding
- Full-colour throughout
- Nutrition information

## Special Occasion Series

- Hardcover concealed wiro
- 8 1/2" x 11" (22 cm x 28 cm) format
- Lay-flat binding
- Full-colour throughout
- Nutrition information

See page 157 for more cookbooks.
For a complete listing, visit
www.companyscoming.com

# Table of Contents

Homemade
Pastas

Beef & Pork

Chicken &
Turkey

Fish & Seafood

Meatless

Salads

Sauces

Sides

# The Company's Coming Story

Jean Paré (pronounced "jeen PAIR-ee") grew up understanding that the combination of family, friends and home cooking is the best recipe for a good life. From her mother, she learned to appreciate good cooking, while her father praised even her earliest attempts in the kitchen. When Jean left home, she took with her a love of cooking, many family recipes and an intriguing desire to read cookbooks as if they were novels!

*"Never share a recipe you wouldn't use yourself."* When her four children had all reached school age, Jean volunteered to cater the 50th anniversary celebration of the Vermilion School of Agriculture, now Lakeland College, in Alberta, Canada. Working out of her home, Jean prepared a dinner for more than 1,000 people, launching a flourishing catering operation that continued for over 18 years. During that time, she had countless opportunities to test new ideas with immediate feedback—resulting in empty plates and contented customers! Whether preparing cocktail sandwiches for a house party or serving a hot meal for 1,500 people, Jean Paré earned a reputation for great food, courteous service and reasonable prices.

As requests for her recipes increased, Jean was often asked the question, "Why don't you write a cookbook?" Jean responded by teaming up with her son, Grant Lovig, in the fall of 1980 to form Company's Coming Publishing Limited. The publication of *150 Delicious Squares* on April 14, 1981 marked the debut of what would soon become one of the world's most popular cookbook series.

The company has grown since those early days when Jean worked from a spare bedroom in her home. Today, she continues to write recipes while working closely with the staff of the Recipe Factory, as the Company's Coming test kitchen is affectionately known. There she fills the role of mentor, assisting with the development of recipes people most want to use for everyday cooking and easy entertaining. Every Company's Coming recipe is kitchen-tested before it is approved for publication.

Jean's daughter, Gail Lovig, is responsible for marketing and distribution, leading a team that includes sales personnel located in major cities across Canada. Company's Coming cookbooks are distributed in Canada, the United States, Australia and other world markets. Bestsellers many times over in English, Company's Coming cookbooks have also been published in French and Spanish.

Familiar and trusted in home kitchens around the world, Company's Coming cookbooks are offered in a variety of formats. Highly regarded as kitchen workbooks, the softcover Original Series, with its lay-flat plastic comb binding, is still a favourite among readers.

Jean Paré's approach to cooking has always called for quick and easy recipes using everyday ingredients. That view has served her well. The recipient of many awards, including the Queen Elizabeth Golden Jubilee Medal, Jean was appointed Member of the Order of Canada, her country's highest lifetime achievement honour.

Jean continues to gain new supporters by adhering to what she calls The Golden Rule of Cooking: *Never share a recipe you wouldn't use yourself.* It's an approach that has worked—millions of times over!

# Foreword

I love pasta! It is truly the busy cook's key to a quick and delicious meal. And really, the combinations of different pastas and sauces are limitless—so dinner will never be boring. It's always a safe bet when you're feeding kids or having guests over, and it's economical to boot!

There are few dishes that can satisfy as well as a plate of pasta with a rich and bold sauce. But pasta isn't only comfort food—it can be eaten as lighter fare in salads or served as an easy side option. How about a lovely Basil Garlic Spaghetti, page 99, tossed with fresh herbs, olives and cherry tomatoes? Done up this way, pasta can make a very light dinner alternative. And now with all the enriched and whole-grain pastas out there, eating pasta will take you a long way towards getting your Health Canada-recommended six to eight grain servings a day.

In *Perfect Pasta And Sauces*, we've created a separate section packed with quick sauce recipes you can make up and serve with the pasta of your choice. Many of the sauces can also be made in bigger batches and stored in the fridge or freezer—perfect when you know you're going to have a busy day!

For those of you who like to get really adventurous, we've even included a section that instructs you on making a variety of different pasta doughs from scratch. And you don't need a pasta machine to make them—although you can certainly use one if you wish. From homemade fettuccine to ravioli to cannelloni, it's easier than you think!

So get that water boiling—it's time to fall in love with pasta all over again!

*Jean Paré*

---

## Nutrition Information Guidelines

Each recipe is analyzed using the most current version of the Canadian Nutrient File from Health Canada, which is based on the United States Department of Agriculture (USDA) Nutrient Database.

- If more than one ingredient is listed (such as "butter or hard margarine"), or if a range is given (1 – 2 tsp., 5 – 10 mL), only the first ingredient or first amount is analyzed.

- For meat, poultry and fish, the serving size per person is based on the recommended 4 oz. (113 g) uncooked weight (without bone), which is 2 – 3 oz. (57 – 85 g) cooked weight (without bone)—approximately the size of a deck of playing cards.

- Milk used is 1% M.F. (milk fat), unless otherwise stated.

- Cooking oil used is canola oil, unless otherwise stated.

- Ingredients indicating "sprinkle," "optional," or "for garnish" are not included in the nutrition information.

- The fat in recipes and combination foods can vary greatly depending on the sources and types of fats used in each specific ingredient. For these reasons, the amount of saturated, monounsaturated and polyunsaturated fats may not add up to the total fat content.

Vera C. Mazurak, Ph.D.
Nutritionist

# It's all in the pasta

*Who says good things don't come easy? Pasta is proof positive that a delicious dinner can be put on the table in mere minutes. And although you may be baffled by the variety available at your local supermarket, when you know the basics a world of pasta possibilities will be at your fingertips.*

## Picking the perfect partner

*The most important rule when pairing sauces with pasta is finding the perfect balance—you don't want your pasta to overwhelm your sauce or vice versa.*

**Lisce versus rigate:** Pasta is either *lisce* (smooth) or *rigate* (ridged) in texture. Smooth pastas do best with more delicate or dryer seasonings and sauces, whereas the ridges in *rigate* pastas are great for holding onto thicker, bolder sauces. If you use a ridged pasta with a delicate sauce, all you'll taste is the pasta, and if you use a smooth, thin pasta with a bold sauce, all you'll taste is the sauce.

**Long versus short:** Because long pasta is generally twirled on a fork, you want to pair it with a sauce that will cling to it. A chunky sauce won't stick to the long pasta during the twirling, so it's better suited to shorter pastas that can be easily picked up with your fork along with pieces of veggies or meat.

**Big versus small:** When working with specially-shaped pastas like bows, spirals, shells or wheels, size can vary drastically. Small shapes are especially great for soups, but the bigger the size, the thicker and chunkier the sauce should be.

**Flavoured versus regular:** Flavoured or herb-flecked pastas are readily available today, and it is important that you keep in mind the pasta's flavour when choosing your sauce. For example, a spinach-flavoured pasta would go very well with a vegetable sauce but may be out of place with a heavy Stroganoff-inspired sauce. Regular pastas are pretty neutral and can be paired with almost anything. And if you are experimenting with whole-wheat, flax or Omega-enriched pastas, consider that they each have their own unique flavours.

## Simple cooking tips to keep them coming back

**Water, water everywhere:** Perhaps the most common mistake people make when cooking pasta is not using enough water. Using too little will make your pasta quite starchy and sticky. Generally, any amount of pasta under 10 oz. (285 g) can be cooked in a large saucepan. If the weight is between 10 and 12.5 oz. (285 – 355 g), use a Dutch oven. Any larger amount will require a large pot, such as a stock pot. Just remember, you can never use too much water.

**Slick trick?:** It is not necessary to add oil to your water when cooking pasta to prevent it from sticking. As long as you use enough water and stir the pasta occasionally, your pasta will be perfect—without any added fat.

**Rolling out the boil:** Only add your pasta to the water when it is at a full boil. This rapid movement will help separate the pasta and keep it from sticking. Also remember to give the pasta a good stir as soon as it's in the water.

**Salty waters:** Adding salt to the water will season the pasta—letting you cut down on the amount of salt used in the sauce.

**Down the drain?:** Rinsing your pasta isn't usually a good idea. It will cool the pasta, making it less absorbent. You want to strain your pasta quickly and immediately mix it with the sauce. If this is done while the pasta is still hot, it will absorb the sauce. The only time you'll want to rinse pasta is when you're making a chilled salad. In that case, rinse with plenty of cold water.

**The *al dente* way:** Pasta that is cooked perfectly is said to be *al dente* (pronounced al-DEN-tay). It is uniform in colour and texture. It isn't crunchy and it isn't mushy—it's tender but firm. The only surefire way of testing doneness is to give it a taste.

**Keeping it fresh:** Dry, uncooked pasta can last for ages if kept in an airtight container, but you'll want to freeze fresh homemade pasta in an airtight container and use within one month. Cooked pasta can also be stored in an airtight container in the fridge but should be used within two days.

## Mixing it up

*Explore all your dinner pastabilities by using a different type of pasta in your favourite recipe. The chart below shows how much dry pasta equals how much cooked pasta and gives general cooking times as well.*

| pasta | raw volume 8 oz. (225 g) | cooked volume | cooking time (min.) |
|---|---|---|---|
| Angel Hair | n/a | 4 cups (1 L) | 3 – 5 |
| Bow, medium | 3 1/3 cups (825 mL) | 4 cups (1 L) | 10 – 12 |
| Cavatappi | 3 cups (750 mL) | 4 cups (1 L) | 10 – 12 |
| Elbow macaroni | 1 3/4 cups (425 mL) | 4 cups (1 L) | 8 – 10 |
| Fettucine | n/a | 3 cups (750 mL) | 11 – 13 |
| Fusilli | 2 2/3 cups (650 mL) | 4 cups (1 L) | 7 – 9 |
| Linguine | n/a | 3 1/2 cups (875 mL) | 9 – 11 |
| Orzo | 1 1/4 cups (300 mL) | 3 cups (750 mL) | 8 – 10 |
| Penne | 2 cups (500 mL) | 3 cups (750 mL) | 14 – 16 |
| Radiatore | 3 1/2 cups (875 mL) | 4 cups (1 L) | 7 – 9 |
| Rigatoni | 3 cups (750 mL) | 5 cups (1.25 L) | 14 – 16 |
| Rotini | 3 cups (750 mL) | 4 cups (1 L) | 12 – 14 |
| Shell, small | 2 1/2 cups (625 mL) | 4 cups (1 L) | 8 – 10 |
| Spaghetti | n/a | 3 cups (750 mL) | 10 – 12 |
| Spaghettini | n/a | 3 cups (750 mL) | 9 – 11 |

## Pasta line-up

*The main types of pasta are string, ribbon, tube, spiral, stuffed and specialty shapes. In this handy go-to glossary we've given you the low-down on the most popular types in each category.*

**Angel hair:** Thin, light and delicate, this long smooth string pasta is good in brothy soups or served with only the most delicate of sauces or seasonings.

**Bow tie (farfalle):** Decorative with a thicker texture, bow-tie pasta is great with bold, chunky sauces. It comes in a range of sizes, from tiny, which is best in soups, to large, which can take on the meatiest, thickest sauces.

**Cannelloni shells:** This large tube pasta is meant to be stuffed and then baked. You can purchase the shells oven-ready, which means the hard shells can be easily stuffed and then put straight in the oven, or you can buy the traditional form, which require cooking before they are stuffed and baked.

**Cavatappi:** This medium-sized, corkscrew pasta is both a tube and a spiral. Its shape is especially good for holding sauces.

**Elbow macaroni:** This common smooth tube pasta is perfect for holding medium-bodied sauces.

**Fettuccine:** This ribbon pasta often comes in flavoured varieties and is perfectly suited to cream or butter-based sauces.

**Fusilli:** This spiral pasta is medium-sized but can vary in the tightness of its spirals. It's quite versatile and lends itself well to vegetable sauces. Rotini is very similar to fusilli, but has tighter spirals.

10

**Lasagna:** This large, flat pasta is always sandwiched between layers of filling before it is baked. This pasta can be purchased oven-ready or in its traditional form which requires cooking before baking.

**Linguine:** This string pasta has a flatter appearance than spaghetti and is used with light to medium-bodied sauces.

**Orzo:** This tiny rice-shaped pasta is most often used in soups.

**Penne:** This tubular pasta can be found in many sizes and with *lisce* or *rigate* textures. Basically, the larger the tubes, the chunkier and meatier the sauces can be.

**Radiatore:** Considered to be shaped like little radiators, this small pasta is good with medium-bodied sauces.

**Rigatoni:** This bigger tube pasta has ridges and is ideal with bold, chunky and meaty sauces.

**Shells:** As its name implies, this pasta is shell-shaped and comes in a variety of sizes. The smallest shells are generally used in soups and jumbo shells are usually stuffed with filling.

**Spaghetti:** Perhaps the most common pasta, spaghetti is a smooth string pasta that is best served with smoother rather than chunkier sauces.

**Spaghettini:** A thinner form of spaghetti, spaghettini is ideal for lighter sauces.

**Tortellini:** Stuffed with cheeses or meats, this medium-sized pasta is usually bought fresh. It is best served with sauces that will highlight rather than compete with its filling.

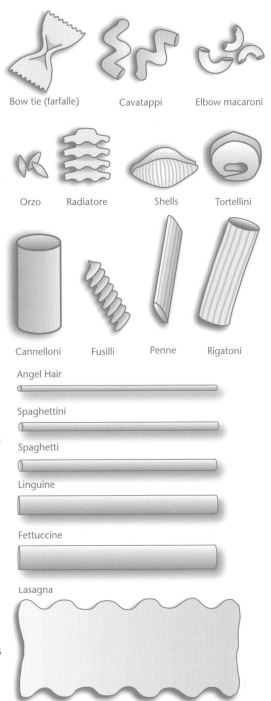

Bow tie (farfalle)   Cavatappi   Elbow macaroni

Orzo   Radiatore   Shells   Tortellini

Cannelloni   Fusilli   Penne   Rigatoni

Angel Hair

Spaghettini

Spaghetti

Linguine

Fettuccine

Lasagna

**11**

# Two-Pepper Gnocchi

*Got gnocchi? With this super-speedy method it'll take no time at all! Red pepper provides a pretty colour while chilies add heat.*

| | | |
|---|---|---|
| Instant potato flakes | 1/3 cup | 75 mL |
| Water | 1/4 cup | 60 mL |
| Large eggs | 2 | 2 |
| Chopped roasted red pepper, drained | 1/4 cup | 60 mL |
| Dried crushed chilies | 1 tsp. | 5 mL |
| Salt | 1/4 tsp. | 1 mL |
| All-purpose flour | 1 1/2 cups | 375 mL |
| All-purpose flour | 1 tbsp. | 15 mL |
| Water | 8 cups | 1 L |
| Salt | 2 tsp. | 10 mL |

Combine potato flakes and water in large bowl. Let stand for 10 minutes. Make a well in centre.

Process next 4 ingredients in blender until smooth. Add to well.

Sprinkle first amount of flour over potato mixture. Mix with fork until mixture starts to come together.

Turn out onto lightly floured surface. Knead gently 6 times until ball forms. Divide into 2 equal portions. Keep remaining portion covered. Roll 1 portion into 3/4 inch (2 cm) thick rope, using second amount of flour as needed to prevent sticking. Cut into 1/2 inch (12 mm) pieces (see Note 1). Arrange gnocchi in single layer on lightly floured baking sheet. Repeat with remaining dough. Makes about 72 gnocchi.

Combine water and salt in Dutch oven. Bring to a boil. Cook gnocchi (see Note 2), in 2 batches, for about 2 minutes, stirring occasionally, until gnocchi float to the top. Cook for 1 minute, before removing with slotted spoon to sieve. Drain. Transfer to serving dish. Cover to keep warm. Makes about 2 1/2 cups (625 mL).

*1 cup (250 mL): 354 Calories; 3.9 g Total Fat (0.1 g Mono, 0.1 g Poly, 1.3 g Sat); 172 mg Cholesterol; 64 g Carbohydrate; 2 g Fibre; 14 g Protein; 578 mg Sodium*

Pictured on page 17.

**Note 1:** If desired, tines of a fork can be gently rolled along gnocchi to create ridges.

*(continued on next page)*

**Note 2:** To store, freeze uncooked gnocchi in a single layer on a lightly floured baking sheet. Store in a resealable freezer bag for up to 3 months. For best results, cook from frozen. Gnocchi can also be pre-cooked, tossed in a little cooking oil or melted butter and chilled. Reheat in boiling water for about 3 minutes. Drain well. Add to your favourite sauce.

# Spinach Pasta Dough

*Think making pasta is hard? This pretty green dough comes together quickly in your food processor for an impressive pasta in no time flat!*

| | | |
|---|---|---|
| Frozen chopped spinach, thawed but not squeezed dry (see Note 1) | 1/2 cup | 125 mL |
| Large egg | 1 | 1 |
| Olive oil | 1 tbsp. | 15 mL |
| Water | 1 tbsp. | 15 mL |
| All-purpose flour | 2 cups | 500 mL |
| Salt | 1/2 tsp. | 2 mL |

Process first 4 ingredients in food processor until smooth.

Gradually add flour and salt, processing with on/off motion until mixture just comes together. Turn out onto lightly floured surface. Knead until ball forms. Wrap with plastic wrap. Let stand for 30 minutes. Divide dough in half. Work with 1 half of dough at a time. Keep remaining half covered with plastic wrap. Roll out dough on lightly floured surface to 16 x 12 inch (40 x 30 cm) rectangle. Loosen and lift dough and sprinkle flour on work surface to prevent sticking. Let stand for 10 minutes. Sprinkle dough with flour. Turn over. Let stand for 10 minutes. To make noodles, fold dough in half lengthwise. Cut crosswise into 1/4 inch (6 mm) wide noodles. Toss gently to loosen. Sprinkle with flour to prevent sticking if necessary. Repeat with remaining dough (see Note 2). Makes about 1 lb. (454 g) uncooked pasta.

*4 oz. (113 g): 255 Calories; 4.7 g Total Fat (2.5 g Mono, 0.5 g Poly, 0.9 g Sat); 54 mg Cholesterol; 45 g Carbohydrate; 2 g Fibre; 8 g Protein; 337 mg Sodium*

**Note 1:** Do not squeeze moisture from spinach. It is used to replace water in this recipe.

**Note 2:** Store uncooked fresh pasta loosely in a covered container in the freezer for up to 1 month. For best results, cook from frozen.

# Basic Potato Gnocchi

*Soft little pillows of potato dough, gnocchi (pronounced NYOH-kee) make a fine base for all kinds of sauces. The flavour is homey and the presentation is rustic, yet interesting. This is pasta of a different kind!*

| | | |
|---|---|---|
| Unpeeled baking potatoes (about 3 medium potatoes) | 1 3/4 lb. | 790 g |
| Large eggs, fork-beaten | 2 | 2 |
| Salt | 1/2 tsp. | 2 mL |
| Pepper | 1/4 tsp. | 1 mL |
| All-purpose flour | 1 1/4 cups | 300 mL |
| Grated Parmesan cheese (optional) | 1/4 cup | 60 mL |
| All-purpose flour | 3 tbsp. | 50 mL |
| Water | 8 cups | 2 L |
| Salt | 2 tsp. | 10 mL |

Bake potatoes in 400°F (205°C) oven for about 45 minutes or boil with skin on until tender. Let stand for 10 minutes until cool enough to handle. Remove peel. Press through coarse sieve or mash well in large bowl (see Note 1). Let stand for about 20 minutes until lukewarm. Make a well in centre.

Add next 3 ingredients to well. Stir.

Sprinkle flour and cheese over potato mixture. Mix lightly with fork until mixture starts to come together.

Turn out onto lightly floured surface. Knead gently 6 times until ball forms. Divide dough into 6 portions. Keep remaining portions covered. Roll 1 portion into 3/4 inch (2 cm) thick rope, using second amount of flour as needed to prevent sticking. Cut into 1/2 inch (12 mm) pieces (see Note 2). Arrange gnocchi in single layer on lightly floured baking sheet. Repeat with remaining dough portions. Makes about 156 gnocchi.

Combine water and salt in Dutch oven. Bring to a boil. Cook gnocchi (see Note 3), in 2 batches, for about 2 minutes, stirring occasionally, until gnocchi float to the top. Cook for 1 minute before removing with slotted spoon to sieve. Drain. Transfer to serving dish. Cover to keep warm. Makes about 4 cups (1 L).

*(continued on next page)*

Homemade Pasta

*1 cup (250 mL): 348 Calories; 2.5 g Total Fat (0 g Mono, 0.1 g Poly, 0.8 g Sat); 108 mg Cholesterol; 72 g Carbohydrate; 5 g Fibre; 11 g Protein; 797 mg Sodium*

Pictured on page 17.

**Note 1:** The finer and fluffier you can mash the cooked potato, the better the texture of the gnocchi.

**Note 2:** If desired, tines of a fork can be gently rolled along gnocchi to create ridges.

**Note 3:** To store, freeze uncooked gnocchi in a single layer on a lightly floured baking sheet. Store in a resealable freezer bag for up to 3 months. For best results, cook from frozen. Gnocchi can also be pre-cooked, tossed in a little cooking oil or melted butter and chilled. Reheat in boiling water for about 3 minutes. Drain well. Add to your favourite sauce.

## Paré Pointer

*All geologists love rock music.*

# Eggless Pasta Dough

*They say you can't make pasta without cracking a few eggs, but we've proved them wrong! This tender, no-egg dough is easy to make and tastes great!*

| | | |
|---|---|---|
| All-purpose flour | 2 cups | 500 mL |
| Salt | 1/2 tsp. | 2 mL |
| Water | 1/2 cup | 125 mL |
| Olive oil | 1 tbsp. | 15 mL |

Combine flour and salt in large bowl. Make a well in centre.

Add water and olive oil to well. Mix until dough begins to come together. Turn out onto lightly floured surface. Knead until ball forms. Wrap with plastic wrap. Let stand for 30 minutes. Divide dough in half. Work with 1 half of dough at a time. Keep remaining half covered with plastic wrap. Roll out dough on lightly floured surface to 16 x 12 inch (40 x 30 cm) rectangle. Loosen and lift dough and sprinkle flour on work surface to prevent sticking. Let stand for 10 minutes. Sprinkle dough with flour. Turn over. Let stand for 10 minutes. To make noodles, fold dough in half lengthwise. Cut crosswise into 1/4 inch (6 mm) wide noodles. Toss gently to loosen. Sprinkle with flour to prevent sticking if necessary. Repeat with remaining dough (see Note). Makes about 1 lb. (454 g) of uncooked pasta.

*4 oz. (113 g): 230 Calories; 3.5 g Total Fat (2.5 g Mono, 0.5 g Poly, 0.5 g Sat); 0 mg Cholesterol; 44 g Carbohydrate; 1 g Fibre; 6 g Protein; 291 mg Sodium*

**Note:** Store uncooked fresh pasta loosely in a covered container in the freezer for up to 1 month. For best results, cook from frozen.

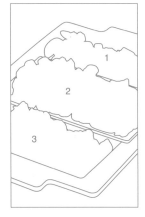

1. Sweet Potato Sage Gnocchi, page 22
2. Basic Potato Gnocchi, page 14, with Parma Rosa Sauce, page 131
3. Two-Pepper Gnocchi, page 12

Props courtesy of: The Bay

# Whole-Wheat Pasta Dough

*This easy-to-make dough comes with whole-grain goodness too!*

| | | |
|---|---|---|
| All-purpose flour | 1 cup | 250 mL |
| Whole-wheat flour | 1 cup | 250 mL |
| Salt | 1/2 tsp. | 2 mL |
| Large eggs, fork-beaten | 2 | 2 |
| Water | 1/4 cup | 60 mL |
| Olive oil | 1 tbsp. | 15 mL |

Combine first 3 ingredients in large bowl. Make a well in centre.

Add remaining 3 ingredients to well. Mix until dough begins to come together. Turn out onto lightly floured surface. Knead until ball forms. Wrap with plastic wrap. Let stand for 30 minutes. Divide dough in half. Work with 1 half of dough at a time. Keep remaining half covered with plastic wrap. Roll out dough on lightly floured surface to 16 x 12 inch (40 x 30 cm) rectangle. Loosen and lift dough and sprinkle flour on work surface to prevent sticking. Let stand for 10 minutes. Sprinkle dough with flour. Turn over. Let stand for 10 minutes. To make noodles, fold dough in half lengthwise. Cut crosswise into 1/4 inch (6 mm) wide noodles. Toss gently to loosen. Sprinkle with flour to prevent sticking if necessary. Repeat with remaining dough (see Note). Makes about 1 lb. (454 g) of uncooked pasta.

*4 oz. (113 g): 267 Calories; 6.3 g Total Fat (2.6 g Mono, 0.7 g Poly, 1.4 g Sat); 108 mg Cholesterol; 44 g Carbohydrate; 4 g Fibre; 10 g Protein; 325 mg Sodium*

**Note:** Store uncooked fresh pasta loosely in a covered container in the freezer for up to 1 month. For best results, cook from frozen.

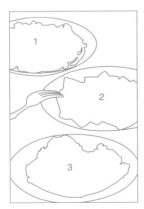

1. Fresh Herb Pasta Dough, page 25
2. Mushroom Ravioli, page 26
3. Pumpkin Cannelloni, page 20

Props courtesy of:   Danesco Inc.
Wal-Mart Canada Inc.

# Pumpkin Cannelloni

*We don't know how to transform a pumpkin into a carriage, but we can use it to make a delicate orange-coloured pasta with a creamy ricotta filling. Try using a rosé or Alfredo sauce for variation.*

| FILLING | | |
|---|---|---|
| Cooking oil | 1 tsp. | 5 mL |
| Chopped onion | 1 cup | 250 mL |
| Garlic cloves, minced | 2 | 2 |
| (or 1/2 tsp., 2 mL, powder) | | |
| Large egg, fork-beaten | 1 | 1 |
| Box of frozen chopped spinach, thawed and squeezed dry | 10 oz. | 300 g |
| Dry curd cottage cheese | 1 cup | 250 mL |
| Ricotta cheese | 1 cup | 250 mL |
| Grated Asiago cheese | 1/2 cup | 125 mL |
| Salt | 1/2 tsp. | 2 mL |
| Pepper | 1/4 tsp. | 1 mL |
| PUMPKIN DOUGH | | |
| All-purpose flour | 2 1/4 cups | 550 mL |
| Salt | 1/2 tsp. | 2 mL |
| Large egg | 1 | 1 |
| Canned pure pumpkin (no spices) | 1/2 cup | 125 mL |
| Olive oil | 1 tbsp. | 15 mL |
| SAUCE | | |
| Tomato pasta sauce | 3 cups | 750 mL |
| Grated Asiago cheese | 1/2 cup | 125 mL |

**Filling:** Heat cooking oil in small frying pan on medium. Add onion and garlic. Cook for 5 to 10 minutes, stirring often, until onion is softened. Transfer to medium bowl.

Add remaining 7 ingredients. Mix well. Set aside.

**Pumpkin Dough:** Combine flour and salt in large bowl. Make a well in centre.

*(continued on next page)*

Homemade Pasta

Whisk next 3 ingredients in small bowl. Add to well. Mix until dough begins to come together. Turn out onto lightly floured surface. Knead until ball forms. Wrap with plastic wrap. Let stand for 30 minutes. Divide dough in half. Work with 1 half of dough at a time. Keep remaining half covered with plastic wrap. Roll out dough on lightly floured surface to 24 x 6 inch (60 x 15 cm) rectangle. Loosen and lift dough and sprinkle flour on work surface to prevent sticking. Let stand for 10 minutes. Sprinkle dough with flour. Turn over. Let stand for 10 minutes. Cut dough into 4 squares, 6 x 6 inches (15 x 15 cm) each. Spread about 1/3 cup (75 mL) filling on each square, leaving 1/2 inch (12 mm) edge from top. Roll up from bottom into a tube to enclose filling.

**Sauce:** Spread 1 cup (250 mL) pasta sauce in bottom of greased 8 x 8 inch (20 x 20 cm) baking dish. Arrange pasta rolls seam-side down over sauce. Cover with remaining sauce. Sprinkle with Asiago cheese. Bake, covered, in 350°F (175°C) oven for 75 minutes until pasta is tender and cheese is melted. Makes 8 cannelloni.

*1 cannelloni: 353 Calories; 13.6 g Total Fat (1.6 g Mono, 0.4 g Poly, 6.2 g Sat); 85 mg Cholesterol; 40 g Carbohydrate; 4 g Fibre; 18 g Protein; 1073 mg Sodium*

Pictured on page 18.

## Paré Pointer

*You can't pay your taxes with a smile. They insist on money.*

# Sweet Potato Sage Gnocchi

*You wouldn't want to cover up the pretty colour and delicate flavour of these dense, flavourful dumplings with a sauce—just a little sage and Parmesan butter is all you need.*

| | | |
|---|---|---|
| Fresh unpeeled orange-fleshed sweet potatoes (about 1 medium sweet potato) | 1 lb. | 454 g |
| Instant potato flakes | 1/2 cup | 125 mL |
| Large egg, fork-beaten | 1 | 1 |
| Garlic powder | 1/8 tsp. | 0.5 mL |
| Salt | 1 tsp. | 5 mL |
| All-purpose flour | 2 cups | 500 mL |
| All-purpose flour | 1/4 cup | 60 mL |
| Water | 12 cups | 3 L |
| Salt | 1 1/2 tsp. | 7 mL |
| Butter (or hard margarine) | 2 tbsp. | 30 mL |
| Grated Parmesan cheese | 1/4 cup | 60 mL |
| Chopped fresh sage | 2 tsp. | 10 mL |

Cut sweet potato in half lengthwise. Place cut-side down on greased baking sheet. Bake in 400°F (205°C) oven for about 40 minutes until tender. Let stand for about 10 minutes until cool enough to handle. Scoop flesh into large bowl. Add potato flakes. Mash (see Note 1). Make a well in centre. Let stand for 10 minutes.

Add next 3 ingredients to well. Stir.

Add first amount of flour. Mix lightly with fork until mixture starts to come together.

Turn out onto lightly floured surface. Knead gently 6 times until ball forms. Divide dough into 4 portions. Keep remaining portions covered. Roll 1 portion into 3/4 inch (2 cm) thick rope, using second amount of flour as needed to prevent sticking. Cut into 1/2 inch (12 mm) pieces (see Note 2). Arrange gnocchi in single layer on lightly floured baking sheet. Repeat with remaining dough portions. Makes about 105 gnocchi.

*(continued on next page)*

Combine water and salt in Dutch oven. Bring to a boil. Cook gnocchi (see Note 3), in 2 batches, for about 2 minutes, stirring occasionally, until gnocchi float to the top. Cook for 1 minute before removing with slotted spoon to sieve. Drain. Transfer to serving dish. Cover to keep warm.

Melt butter in large frying pan on medium. Add gnocchi. Sprinkle with cheese and sage. Heat and stir for about 2 minutes until heated through. Makes about 4 1/2 cups (1.1 L).

*1 cup (250 mL): 372 Calories; 8.3 g Total Fat (1.4 g Mono, 0.3 g Poly, 4.9 g Sat); 68 mg Cholesterol; 63 g Carbohydrate; 4 g Fibre; 12 g Protein; 1023 mg Sodium*

Pictured on page 17.

**Note 1:** You should have about 1 1/4 cups (300 mL) mashed sweet potato.

**Note 2:** If desired, tines of a fork can be gently rolled along gnocchi to create ridges.

**Note 3:** To store, freeze uncooked gnocchi in a single layer on a lightly floured baking sheet. Store in a resealable freezer bag for up to 3 months. For best results, cook from frozen. Gnocchi can also be pre-cooked, tossed in a little cooking oil or melted butter and chilled. Reheat in boiling water for about 3 minutes. Drain well. Add butter mixture.

## Paré Pointer

*If you find your goat eating a dictionary, take the words right out of his mouth.*

# Chili Pasta Dough

*It's not sauce that adds spice to this pasta—it's the jalapeño peppers mixed right into the dough!*

| All-purpose flour | 2 cups | 500 mL |
| Salt | 1/4 tsp. | 1 mL |
| | | |
| Large eggs | 2 | 2 |
| Water | 1/4 cup | 60 mL |
| Chopped pickled jalapeño peppers | 2 tbsp. | 30 mL |
| Olive oil | 1 tbsp. | 15 mL |

Combine flour and salt in large bowl. Make a well in centre.

Process remaining 4 ingredients in blender until smooth. Add to well. Mix until dough begins to come together. Turn out onto lightly floured surface. Knead until ball forms. Wrap with plastic wrap. Let stand for 30 minutes. Divide dough in half. Work with 1 half of dough at a time. Keep remaining half covered with plastic wrap. Roll out dough on lightly floured surface to 16 x 12 inch (40 x 30 cm) rectangle. Loosen and lift dough and sprinkle flour on work surface to prevent sticking. Let stand for 10 minutes. Sprinkle dough with flour. Turn over. Let stand for 10 minutes. To make noodles, fold dough in half lengthwise. Cut crosswise into 1/4 inch (6 mm) wide noodles. Toss gently to loosen. Sprinkle with flour to prevent sticking if necessary. Repeat with remaining dough (see Note). Makes about 1 lb. (454 g) uncooked pasta.

*4 oz. (113 g): 268 Calories; 5.8 g Total Fat (2.5 g Mono, 0.5 g Poly, 1.3 g Sat); 108 mg Cholesterol; 45 g Carbohydrate; 1 g Fibre; 9 g Protein; 238 mg Sodium*

**Note:** Store uncooked fresh pasta loosely in a covered container in the freezer for up to 1 month. For best results, cook from frozen.

**SESAME CHILI PASTA DOUGH:** Instead of olive oil, use same amount of sesame oil.

# Fresh Herb Pasta Dough

*Fresh herbs add rich flavour to this colourful homemade pasta. This is one pasta that is just as good with or without sauce!*

| All-purpose flour | 2 cups | 500 mL |
| Salt | 1/2 tsp. | 2 mL |
| | | |
| Large eggs, fork-beaten | 2 | 2 |
| Water | 1/4 cup | 60 mL |
| Chopped fresh basil | 2 tbsp. | 30 mL |
| Chopped fresh oregano | 1 tbsp. | 15 mL |
| Olive oil | 1 tbsp. | 15 mL |
| Fresh thyme leaves | 2 tsp. | 10 mL |
| Chopped fresh rosemary | 1 tsp. | 5 mL |

Combine flour and salt in large bowl. Make a well in centre.

Process remaining 7 ingredients in blender. Add to well. Mix until dough begins to come together. Turn out onto lightly floured surface. Knead until ball forms. Wrap with plastic wrap. Let stand for 30 minutes. Divide dough in half. Work with 1 half of dough at a time. Keep remaining half covered with plastic wrap. Roll out dough on lightly floured surface to 16 x 12 inch (40 x 30 cm) rectangle. Loosen and lift dough and sprinkle flour on work surface to prevent sticking. Let stand for 10 minutes. Sprinkle dough with flour. Turn over. Let stand for 10 minutes. To make noodles, fold dough in half lengthwise. Cut crosswise into 1/4 inch (6 mm) wide noodles. Toss gently to loosen. Sprinkle with flour to prevent sticking if necessary. Repeat with remaining dough (see Note). Makes about 1 lb. (454 g) uncooked pasta.

*4 oz (113 g): 267 Calories; 5.8 g Total Fat (2.5 g Mono, 0.5 g Poly, 1.3 g Sat); 108 mg Cholesterol; 45 g Carbohydrate; 1 g Fibre; 9.1 g Protein; 323 mg Sodium*

Pictured on page 18.

**Note:** Store uncooked fresh pasta loosely in a covered container in the freezer for up to 1 month. For best results, cook from frozen.

**LEMON THYME PASTA DOUGH:** Omit basil, oregano and rosemary. Use 1 tbsp. (15 mL) fresh thyme, 1 tbsp. (15 mL) grated lemon zest and 1 tsp. (5 mL) lemon juice.

**BASIL PEPPER PASTA DOUGH:** Omit oregano, thyme and rosemary. Use 1 tbsp. (15 mL) chopped fresh basil and 2 tsp. (10 mL) pepper.

# Mushroom Ravioli

*For an elegant and delicious meal, you can't beat homemade ravioli in a rich cream sauce. A bit labour-intensive, but the end result is more than worth it!*

### FILLING

| | | |
|---|---|---|
| Cooking oil | 1 tsp. | 5 mL |
| Chopped fresh white mushrooms | 1 1/2 cups | 375 mL |
| Chopped onion | 1/2 cup | 125 mL |
| Chopped red pepper | 1/2 cup | 125 mL |
| All-purpose flour | 2 tsp. | 10 mL |
| Garlic powder | 1/4 tsp. | 1 mL |
| Italian seasoning | 1/4 tsp. | 1 mL |
| Salt | 1/4 tsp. | 1 mL |
| Pepper | 1/8 tsp. | 0.5 mL |
| Ricotta cheese | 1/2 cup | 125 mL |

### PAPRIKA PASTA DOUGH

| | | |
|---|---|---|
| All-purpose flour | 2 cups | 500 mL |
| Paprika | 1/2 tsp. | 2 mL |
| Salt | 1/2 tsp. | 2 mL |
| Large eggs, fork-beaten | 2 | 2 |
| Water | 1/4 cup | 60 mL |
| Olive oil | 1 tbsp. | 15 mL |
| Large egg, fork-beaten | 1 | 1 |

### SAUCE

| | | |
|---|---|---|
| Butter (or hard margarine) | 2 tbsp. | 30 mL |
| All-purpose flour | 2 tbsp. | 30 mL |
| Milk | 2 cups | 500 mL |
| Italian seasoning | 1/2 tsp. | 2 mL |
| Salt | 1/2 tsp. | 2 mL |
| Pepper | 1/8 tsp. | 0.5 mL |
| Water | 12 cups | 3 L |
| Salt | 1 1/2 tsp. | 7 mL |

*(continued on next page)*

Homemade Pasta

**Filling:** Heat cooking oil in large frying pan on medium. Add mushrooms and onion. Cook for 5 to 10 minutes, stirring occasionally, until onion is softened.

Add next 6 ingredients. Stir. Cook for 3 to 5 minutes until red pepper is tender-crisp.

Add ricotta cheese. Stir. Set aside.

**Paprika Pasta Dough:** Combine first 3 ingredients in large bowl. Make a well in centre.

Add next 3 ingredients to well. Mix until dough begins to come together. Turn out onto lightly floured surface. Knead until ball forms. Wrap with plastic wrap. Let stand for 30 minutes. Divide dough in half. Work with 1 half of dough at a time. Keep remaining half covered with plastic wrap. Roll out dough on lightly floured surface to 16 x 12 inch (40 x 30 cm) rectangle. Loosen and lift dough and sprinkle flour on work surface to prevent sticking. Let stand for 10 minutes. Sprinkle dough with flour. Turn over. Let stand for 10 minutes. Cut both sheets of dough into 2 x 2 inch (5 x 5 cm) squares. Place about 1 tsp. (5 mL) of filling on half of squares.

Brush edges with egg. Cover filling with remaining squares. Press edges to seal, squeezing out any excess air. Makes about 48 ravioli.

**Sauce:** Melt butter in medium saucepan on medium. Add flour. Heat and stir for 1 minute.

Slowly add milk, stirring constantly, until smooth. Add next 3 ingredients. Heat and stir for about 5 minutes until boiling and thickened.

Combine water and salt in Dutch oven. Bring to a boil. Add 1/3 of ravioli. Boil, uncovered, for about 5 minutes, stirring occasionally, until tender but firm. Transfer with slotted spoon to sieve. Drain. Transfer to serving bowl. Cover to keep warm. Repeat with remaining ravioli. Serve with sauce. Serves 4.

*1 serving: 485 Calories; 18.6 g Total Fat (5.2 g Mono, 1.1 g Poly, 8.3 g Sat); 196 mg Cholesterol; 59 g Carbohydrate; 2 g Fibre; 20 g Protein; 934 mg Sodium*

Pictured on page 18.

 To julienne, cut into very thin strips that resemble matchsticks.

# Beef Spaghetti Pie

*This is not your typical pie! A golden-brown spaghetti "crust" is topped with
rosemary-flavoured meat sauce and plenty of cheese.*

| | | |
|---|---|---|
| Water | 8 cups | 2 L |
| Salt | 1 tsp. | 5 mL |
| Spaghetti | 6 oz. | 170 g |
| Grated Parmesan cheese | 1/2 cup | 125 mL |
| Ricotta cheese | 1/2 cup | 125 mL |
| Cooking oil | 2 tsp. | 10 mL |
| Lean ground beef | 1 lb. | 454 g |
| Chopped onion | 1 cup | 250 mL |
| Garlic clove, minced | 1 | 1 |
| (or 1/4 tsp., 1 mL, powder) | | |
| Tomato pasta sauce | 1 1/2 cups | 375 mL |
| Chopped fresh rosemary | 2 tsp. | 10 mL |
| Grated mozzarella cheese | 1 cup | 250 mL |

Combine water and salt in large saucepan. Bring to a boil. Add pasta.
Boil, uncovered, for 10 to 12 minutes, stirring occasionally, until tender
but firm. Drain. Return to same pot.

Add Parmesan cheese. Toss. Pack into bottom of greased 9 inch (22 cm)
deep dish pie plate.

Spread ricotta cheese over pasta mixture.

Heat cooking oil in large frying pan on medium. Add next 3 ingredients.
Scramble-fry for about 10 minutes until no longer pink.

Add pasta sauce and rosemary. Stir. Spoon evenly over ricotta.

Sprinkle with mozzarella cheese. Bake, uncovered, in 325°F (160°C) oven
for about 25 minutes until cheese is melted. Let stand for 10 minutes. Cuts
into 6 wedges.

*1 wedge: 402 Calories; 16.5 g Total Fat (4.2 g Mono, 0.7 g Poly, 7.4 g Sat); 71 mg Cholesterol;
31 g Carbohydrate; 2 g Fibre; 32 g Protein; 687 mg Sodium*

# Fettuccine Stroganoff

*This rich and creamy stroganoff is comfort food at its best. The perfect pairing for tender pasta.*

| | | |
|---|---|---|
| Cooking oil | 2 tsp. | 10 mL |
| Beef top sirloin steak, sliced diagonally across the grain into 1/8 inch (3 mm) thick slices | 1 lb. | 454 g |
| Thinly sliced onion | 1 cup | 250 mL |
| Garlic clove, minced (or 1/4 tsp., 1 mL, powder) | 1 | 1 |
| Sliced fresh white mushrooms | 3 cups | 750 mL |
| Paprika | 1 tsp. | 5 mL |
| Pepper | 1/4 tsp. | 1 mL |
| All-purpose flour | 1 tbsp. | 15 mL |
| Prepared beef broth | 2 cups | 500 mL |
| Water | 12 cups | 3 L |
| Salt | 1 1/2 tsp. | 7 mL |
| Fettuccine | 8 oz. | 225 g |
| Sour cream | 1 cup | 250 mL |

Heat cooking oil in large frying pan on medium-high. Add beef. Stir-fry for about 5 minutes until starting to turn brown. Remove with slotted spoon to plate. Cover to keep warm. Reduce heat to medium.

Add onion and garlic to same frying pan. Cook for 3 to 5 minutes, stirring occasionally, until onion starts to soften.

Add next 3 ingredients. Cook for about 5 minutes, stirring occasionally, until liquid is evaporated.

Add flour. Heat and stir for 1 minute. Add broth. Heat and stir until boiling and thickened. Add beef. Stir. Reduce heat to medium. Simmer, uncovered, for about 10 minutes until beef is tender.

Combine water and salt in Dutch oven. Bring to a boil. Add pasta. Boil, uncovered, for 11 to 13 minutes, stirring occasionally, until tender but firm. Drain. Add to beef mixture. Stir.

Add sour cream. Heat and stir until heated through. Makes about 6 cups (1.5 L).

*1 cup (250 mL): 384 Calories; 14.6 g Total Fat (3.2 g Mono, 0.7 g Poly, 7.0 g Sat); 67 mg Cholesterol; 36 g Carbohydrate; 2 g Fibre; 24 g Protein; 504 mg Sodium*

Beef & Pork

# Greco Beef Manicotti

*Craving Greek? How about Italian? Have a little of each with these pasta rolls filled with great Mediterranean flavours. Serve with a Greek salad and some crusty bread.*

| | | |
|---|---|---|
| Olive (or cooking) oil | 1 tbsp. | 15 mL |
| Lean ground beef | 1 lb. | 454 g |
| Chopped onion | 1 cup | 250 mL |
| Garlic clove, minced (or 1/4 tsp., 1 mL, powder) | 1 | 1 |
| Sliced black olives | 1/2 cup | 125 mL |
| Crumbled feta cheese | 1/3 cup | 75 mL |
| Tomato pasta sauce | 1/4 cup | 60 mL |
| Sun-dried tomato pesto | 2 tbsp. | 30 mL |
| Dried oregano | 1 1/2 tsp. | 7 mL |
| Grated lemon zest | 1 tsp. | 5 mL |
| Tomato pasta sauce | 1 cup | 250 mL |
| Fresh lasagna sheets (about 6 x 8 inches, 15 x 20 cm, each), see Note | 4 | 4 |
| Tomato pasta sauce | 2 cups | 500 mL |
| Crumbled feta cheese | 1/3 cup | 75 mL |
| Chopped fresh basil | 2 tbsp. | 30 mL |

Heat olive oil in large frying pan on medium. Add next 3 ingredients. Scramble-fry for about 10 minutes until beef is no longer pink and onion is softened.

Add next 6 ingredients. Stir.

Spread first amount of pasta sauce on bottom of greased 8 x 8 inch (20 x 20 cm) baking dish.

Soak pasta sheets in warm water for 2 minutes to soften. Blot dry. Spread about 3/4 cup (175 mL) beef mixture over each pasta sheet, leaving 1/2 inch (12 mm) along one longer edge. Roll up, jelly roll-style, from opposite long edge.

*(continued on next page)*

Beef & Pork

Arrange rolls, seam-side down, close together in baking dish. Pour second amount of pasta sauce over rolls. Bake, covered, in 350°F (175°C) oven for about 75 minutes until pasta is tender. Let stand, uncovered, for 10 minutes.

Sprinkle with second amount of cheese and basil. Makes 4 manicotti.

*1 manicotti: 529 Calories; 24.0 g Total Fat (9.9 g Mono, 1.2 g Poly, 9.1 g Sat); 96 mg Cholesterol; 46 g Carbohydrate; 6 g Fibre; 33 g Protein; 1746 mg Sodium*

Pictured on page 36.

**Note:** You may use a fresh homemade pasta instead of purchased pasta sheets. Roll pasta out into four 6 x 8 inch (15 x 20 cm) rectangles.

### Paré Pointer

*If you crossed a canary and an alley cat, would you have a peeping tom?*

# Sweet-And-Spicy Pork

*How did angel hair pasta get its name? We figure it's because it tastes so heavenly! Here, we've tossed it with juicy pork, veggies and a spicy, tangy sauce.*

| | | |
|---|---|---|
| Water | 8 cups | 2 L |
| Salt | 1 tsp. | 5 mL |
| Angel hair pasta, broken into thirds | 8 oz. | 225 g |
| Fresh bean sprouts | 2 cups | 500 mL |
| Pork tenderloin, trimmed of fat, halved lengthwise and cut into 1/4 inch (6 mm) thick slices | 3/4 lb. | 340 g |
| Sesame oil (for flavour) | 2 tsp. | 10 mL |
| Seasoned salt | 1 tsp. | 5 mL |
| Cooking oil | 2 tsp. | 10 mL |
| Thinly sliced red pepper | 2 cups | 500 mL |
| Thinly sliced onion | 1 cup | 250 mL |
| Garlic cloves, minced (or 1/2 tsp., 2 mL, powder) | 2 | 2 |
| Sweet chili sauce | 1/3 cup | 75 mL |
| Lime juice | 3 tbsp. | 50 mL |
| Brown sugar, packed | 2 tbsp. | 30 mL |
| Soy sauce | 2 tbsp. | 30 mL |
| Chili paste (sambal oelek) | 1/2 tsp. | 2 mL |
| Pepper | 1/4 tsp. | 1 mL |

Combine water and salt in Dutch oven. Bring to a boil. Add pasta. Boil, uncovered, for 3 to 5 minutes, stirring occasionally, until tender but firm.

Add bean sprouts. Stir. Cook, uncovered, for 15 seconds. Drain. Return to same pot. Cover to keep warm.

Combine next 3 ingredients in medium bowl.

Heat cooking oil in large frying pan on medium. Add next 3 ingredients and pork mixture. Cook for about 10 minutes until pork is browned.

Add remaining 6 ingredients. Heat and stir for 2 to 4 minutes until slightly thickened. Add to pasta mixture. Toss. Makes about 7 cups (1.75 L).

*1 cup (250 mL): 281 Calories; 5.1 g Total Fat (1.5 g Mono, 0.7 g Poly, 0.9 g Sat); 32 mg Cholesterol; 42 g Carbohydrate; 2 g Fibre; 17 g Protein; 720 mg Sodium*

Beef & Pork

# Meaty Macaroni Pizza

*There's no need to knead or rise, just replace pizza dough with a pasta surprise! Crisp on the outside, chewy within—use your favourite toppings and watch the kids grin!*

| | | |
|---|---|---|
| Water | 8 cups | 2 L |
| Salt | 1 tsp. | 5 mL |
| Elbow macaroni | 2 cups | 500 mL |
| Large eggs | 2 | 2 |
| Milk | 1/2 cup | 125 mL |
| Onion salt | 1/4 tsp. | 1 mL |
| Barbecue sauce | 1 cup | 250 mL |
| Grated Parmesan cheese | 1/4 cup | 60 mL |
| Deli roast beef slices, cut into thin strips | 2 oz. | 57 g |
| Deli ham slices, cut into thin strips | 2 oz. | 57 g |
| Grated mozzarella cheese | 3/4 cup | 175 mL |
| Deli chicken breast slices, cut into thin strips | 2 oz. | 57 g |
| Deli pepperoni slices | 2 oz. | 57 g |
| Sliced green onion | 1/2 cup | 125 mL |
| Grated mozzarella cheese | 3/4 cup | 175 mL |

Combine water and salt in large saucepan. Bring to a boil. Add pasta. Boil, uncovered, for 8 to 10 minutes, stirring occasionally, until tender but firm. Drain. Return to same pot.

Beat next 3 ingredients in small bowl until smooth. Add to pasta. Stir well. Spread on greased 12 inch (30 cm) pizza pan. Bake, uncovered, in 350°F (175°C) oven for about 10 minutes until set.

Spread barbecue sauce over pasta crust. Sprinkle with Parmesan cheese.

Layer next 6 ingredients, in order given, over Parmesan cheese.

Sprinkle with second amount of mozzarella cheese. Bake, uncovered, for about 10 minutes until hot and cheese is melted. Cuts into 8 wedges.

*1 wedge: 256 Calories; 8.1 g Total Fat (0.3 g Mono, 0.2 g Poly, 3.1 g Sat); 77 mg Cholesterol; 28 g Carbohydrate; 1 g Fibre; 18 g Protein; 819 mg Sodium*

# Quick Meatball Casserole

*In a hurry? Grab a few items from your freezer and pantry and you'll be well on your way to a family-friendly dinner. Try with salsa instead of sauce and Mexican cheese blend for a fiesta kick!*

| | | |
|---|---|---|
| Water | 8 cups | 2 L |
| Salt | 1 tsp. | 5 mL |
| Cavatappi pasta | 3 cups | 750 mL |
| Chunky tomato pasta sauce | 2 1/2 cups | 625 mL |
| Frozen cooked meatballs, thawed | 24 | 24 |
| Finely chopped green pepper | 1/2 cup | 125 mL |
| Grated Italian cheese blend | 1 1/2 cups | 375 mL |

Combine water and salt in large saucepan. Bring to a boil. Add pasta. Boil, uncovered, for 8 minutes, stirring occasionally. Drain, reserving 1 cup (250 mL) cooking water. Return pasta and cooking water to same pot.

Add next 3 ingredients. Stir. Transfer to greased 2 quart (2 L) casserole. Bake, covered, in 375°F (190°C) oven for 30 minutes.

Sprinkle with cheese. Bake, uncovered, for about 15 minutes until bubbling and cheese is melted. Serves 4.

*1 serving: 735 Calories; 33.4 g Total Fat (9.4 g Mono, 1.1 g Poly, 13.9 g Sat); 170 mg Cholesterol; 64 g Carbohydrate; 3 g Fibre; 48 g Protein; 983 mg Sodium*

1. Beef Satay Linguine, page 46
2. Curried Pork And Veggies, page 42
3. Spicy Sausage Ratatouille, page 44

Props courtesy of: Pfaltzgraff Canada
 Cherison Enterprises Inc.

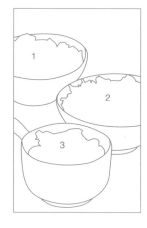

# Bacon Mushroom Spirals

*With rich cheese, bacon and mushrooms, this isn't only comfort food—it's a treat!*

| | | |
|---|---|---|
| Water | 12 cups | 3 L |
| Salt | 1 1/2 tsp. | 7 mL |
| Cavatappi pasta | 4 cups | 1 L |
| Egg yolks (large), fork-beaten | 2 | 2 |
| Grated Parmesan cheese | 1/2 cup | 125 mL |
| Coarsely ground pepper | 1/2 tsp. | 2 mL |
| Bacon slices, diced | 8 | 8 |
| Sliced fresh brown (or white) mushrooms | 3 cups | 750 mL |
| Dried crushed chilies (optional) | 1/2 tsp. | 2 mL |
| Evaporated milk | 1 cup | 250 mL |

Chopped fresh parsley, for garnish

Combine water and salt in Dutch oven. Bring to a boil. Add pasta. Boil, uncovered, for 10 to 12 minutes, stirring occasionally, until tender but firm. Drain, reserving 1/2 cup (125 mL) cooking water.

Meanwhile, combine next 3 ingredients in small bowl. Set aside.

Cook bacon in large frying pan on medium-high, stirring occasionally, until almost crisp. Drain all but 1 tbsp. (15 mL) drippings. Reduce heat to medium. Add mushrooms and chilies. Cook for about 5 minutes, stirring occasionally, until liquid has evaporated.

Add evaporated milk. Reduce heat to medium-low. Cook for about 5 minutes, stirring occasionally, until mixture thickens. Add pasta, reserved cooking water and egg mixture. Heat and stir for 1 minute.

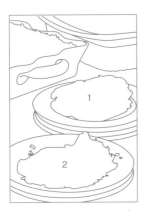

Sprinkle with parsley. Makes about 6 cups (1.5 L).

*1 cup (250 mL): 340 Calories; 13.4 g Total Fat (3.7 g Mono, 1.0 g Poly, 6.7 g Sat); 103 mg Cholesterol; 38 g Carbohydrate; 2 g Fibre; 17 g Protein; 415 mg Sodium*

1. Pesto Olive Lasagna, page 48
2. Greco Beef Manicotti, page 30

Props courtesy of: Danesco Inc.
Corningware®

# Meat Sauce And Radiatore Bake

*Rich, hearty meat sauce and crinkly pasta spirals are topped with a golden-brown blanket of melted cheese.*

| | | |
|---|---|---|
| Cooking oil | 2 tsp. | 10 mL |
| Hot Italian sausage, casing removed | 6 oz. | 170 g |
| Lean ground pork | 6 oz. | 170 g |
| Sliced fresh white mushrooms | 2 cups | 500 mL |
| Chopped onion | 1/2 cup | 125 mL |
| Dried basil | 1 tbsp. | 15 mL |
| Dried oregano | 1 tbsp. | 15 mL |
| Garlic clove, minced | 1 | 1 |
| (or 1/4 tsp., 1 mL, powder) | | |
| Tomato pasta sauce | 3 cups | 750 mL |
| Can of diced tomatoes (with juice) | 14 oz. | 398 mL |
| Granulated sugar | 2 tsp. | 10 mL |
| Salt | 1/4 tsp. | 1 mL |
| Pepper | 1/4 tsp. | 1 mL |
| Water | 12 cups | 3 L |
| Salt | 1 1/2 tsp. | 7 mL |
| Radiatore pasta | 3 cups | 750 mL |
| Grated Italian cheese blend | 1 cup | 250 mL |
| Grated Italian cheese blend | 1 cup | 250 mL |

Heat cooking oil in large frying pan on medium. Add sausage and pork. Scramble-fry for about 10 minutes until no longer pink. Drain. Add next 5 ingredients. Cook for about 10 minutes, stirring occasionally, until onion is softened.

Add next 5 ingredients. Stir. Bring to a boil. Reduce heat to medium-low. Simmer, covered, for 10 minutes to blend flavours.

Combine water and salt in Dutch oven. Bring to a boil. Add pasta. Boil, uncovered, for 5 minutes, stirring occasionally. Drain.

Add pasta and first amount of cheese to meat sauce. Stir. Transfer to greased 2 quart (2 L) casserole.

Sprinkle with second amount of cheese. Bake, covered, in 350°F (175°C) oven for about 40 minutes until bubbling and cheese is melted. Serves 4.

*1 serving: 662 Calories; 31 g Total Fat (7.1 g Mono, 1.7 g Poly, 12.8 g Sat); 81 mg Cholesterol; 64 g Carbohydrate; 6 g Fibre; 36 g Protein; 1961 mg Sodium*

# Pan Perogy

*Love perogies, but don't have the time to make them? Try this incredibly easy,*
*lasagna-style casserole instead. Serve with a tossed salad or steamed vegetables.*

| | | |
|---|---|---|
| Water | 12 cups | 3 L |
| Salt | 1 1/2 tsp. | 7 mL |
| Lasagna noodles | 12 | 12 |
| Bacon slices, finely diced | 8 | 8 |
| Coleslaw mix | 8 cups | 2 L |
| Chopped onion | 2 cups | 500 mL |
| Mashed potatoes (see Note) | 2 cups | 500 mL |
| Mashed potatoes (see Note) | 2 cups | 500 mL |
| 2% cottage cheese, mashed | 1/2 cup | 125 mL |
| Onion salt | 1/2 tsp. | 2 mL |
| Pepper | 1/8 tsp. | 0.5 mL |
| Grated medium Cheddar cheese | 2 cups | 500 mL |

Combine water and salt in Dutch oven. Bring to a boil. Add noodles. Boil, uncovered, for about 12 minutes, stirring occasionally, until tender but firm. Drain. Rinse with cold water. Drain. Line bottom of greased 9 x 13 inch (22 x 33 cm) baking dish with 4 noodles. Set aside.

Cook bacon in large frying pan on medium until almost crisp.

Add coleslaw mix and onion. Cook for about 10 minutes, stirring often, until onion is softened. Remove from heat. Transfer half of coleslaw mixture to large bowl. Set aside remaining half.

Add first amount of mashed potatoes to coleslaw mixture in bowl. Stir. Spread over noodles in pan. Arrange 4 noodles over top.

Combine next 4 ingredients in same bowl. Spread over noodles in pan. Arrange remaining 4 noodles over top. Scatter remaining coleslaw mixture over top.

Sprinkle with Cheddar cheese. Bake, covered, in 350°F (175°C) oven for about 1 hour until heated through. Let stand for 10 minutes. Cuts into 8 pieces.

*1 piece: 486 Calories; 20.8 g Total Fat (7.3 g Mono, 1.6 g Poly, 9.6 g Sat); 46 mg Cholesterol;*
*56 g Carbohydrate; 6 g Fibre; 19 g Protein; 883 mg Sodium*

**Note:** Use about 2 lbs. (900 g) uncooked potatoes to yield 4 cups (1 L) cooked mashed potato.

# Family Lasagna

*Your family deserves the best lasagna! Family Meat Sauce,*
*page 132 (or your favourite), combined with a cheesy cream sauce, provides*
*hearty flavour and rich texture. This lovely layered delight is sure to*
*appeal to kids and grown-ups alike.*

| | | |
|---|---|---|
| Water | 12 cups | 3 L |
| Salt | 1 1/2 tsp. | 7 mL |
| Lasagna noodles | 12 | 12 |
| Butter (or hard margarine) | 3 tbsp. | 50 mL |
| All-purpose flour | 3 tbsp. | 50 mL |
| Salt | 1/2 tsp. | 2 mL |
| Pepper | 1/2 tsp. | 2 mL |
| Nutmeg, just a pinch | | |
| Milk | 2 cups | 500 mL |
| Grated sharp Cheddar cheese | 1/2 cup | 125 mL |
| Family Meat Sauce (page 132) | 4 cups | 1 L |
| Grated mozzarella cheese | 3 cups | 750 mL |
| Grated Parmesan cheese | 1/2 cup | 125 mL |

Combine water and salt in Dutch oven. Bring to a boil. Add noodles. Boil, uncovered, for 12 to 15 minutes, stirring occasionally, until tender but firm. Drain. Rinse with cold water. Drain well.

Melt butter in medium saucepan on medium. Add next 4 ingredients. Heat and stir for 1 minute.

Slowly add milk, stirring constantly, until smooth. Heat and stir for about 5 minutes until boiling and thickened. Remove from heat.

Add Cheddar cheese. Stir until melted. To assemble, layer ingredients in greased 9 x 13 inch (22 x 33 cm) baking dish as follows:

1. 4 noodles
2. 1/3 of meat sauce
3. 1/3 of cheese sauce
4. 4 noodles
5. 1/3 of meat sauce

*(continued on next page)*

6. 1/3 of cheese sauce
7. Remaining 4 noodles
8. Remaining meat sauce
9. Remaining cheese sauce

Sprinkle with mozzarella and Parmesan cheese. Bake, uncovered, in 350°F (175°C) oven for about 45 minutes until heated through and cheese is melted and golden. Cuts into 8 pieces.

*1 piece:* 413 Calories; 16.1 g Total Fat (3.6 g Mono, 0.5 g Poly, 8.9 g Sat); 58 mg Cholesterol; 37 g Carbohydrate; 2 g Fibre; 31 g Protein; 982 mg Sodium

**Variation:** This recipe works great with spinach or whole-wheat lasagna noodles in place of regular.

**TEX-MEX FAMILY LASAGNA:** Instead of sharp Cheddar cheese and mozzarella cheese, use the same amounts of grated Mexican cheese blend.

**SPEEDY FAMILY LASAGNA:** Save yourself some time! Instead of making the homemade cheese sauce, use 2 1/4 cups (550 mL) store-bought alfredo sauce.

## Paré Pointer

*Every archaeologist's career is in ruins*

# Curried Pork And Veggies

*Veggies and spice, and everything nice—that's what great meals are made of!*
*A hearty one-dish dinner with nothing else required but a nice glass of wine.*

| | | |
|---|---|---|
| Water | 8 cups | 2 L |
| Salt | 1 tsp. | 5 mL |
| Angel hair pasta, broken in half | 6 oz. | 170 g |
| Julienned carrot (see Tip, page 27) | 1 cup | 250 mL |
| Cooking oil | 2 tsp. | 10 mL |
| Lean ground pork | 1 lb. | 454 g |
| Garlic cloves, minced | 2 | 2 |
| (or 1/2 tsp., 2 mL, powder) | | |
| Curry powder | 2 tsp. | 10 mL |
| Ground ginger | 2 tsp. | 10 mL |
| Dried crushed chilies | 1/2 tsp. | 2 mL |
| Sliced fresh white mushrooms | 2 cups | 500 mL |
| Thinly sliced green pepper | 1/4 cup | 60 mL |
| Thinly sliced red pepper | 1/4 cup | 60 mL |
| Can of condensed chicken broth | 10 oz. | 284 mL |
| Soy sauce | 2 tbsp. | 30 mL |
| Cornstarch | 1 tbsp. | 15 mL |
| Brown sugar, packed | 1 tsp. | 5 mL |
| Fresh bean sprouts | 2 cups | 500 mL |
| Sliced green onion | 3/4 cup | 175 mL |

Combine water and salt in large saucepan. Bring to a boil. Add pasta. Boil, uncovered, for 2 minutes, stirring occasionally. Add carrot. Cook, uncovered, for 3 minutes, stirring occasionally, until pasta is tender but firm. Drain. Return to same pot. Cover to keep warm.

Heat cooking oil in large frying pan on medium. Add next 5 ingredients. Scramble-fry for 8 to 10 minutes until browned.

Add next 3 ingredients. Cook and stir for about 3 minutes until peppers are softened.

Stir next 4 ingredients in small bowl until smooth. Add to pork mixture. Heat and stir for 3 to 5 minutes until boiling and thickened.

Add bean sprouts, green onion and pasta mixture. Stir until heated through. Makes about 8 cups (2 L).

*(continued on next page)*

Beef & Pork

Pictured on page 35.

# Teriyaki Beef Rotini

*Think the tang of teriyaki is only suited to stir-fries? Here we've used it to infuse this beefy rotini with great Asian flavour.*

| | | |
|---|---|---|
| Water | 8 cups | 2 L |
| Salt | 1 tsp. | 5 mL |
| Rotini pasta | 3 cups | 750 mL |
| Cooking oil | 2 tsp. | 10 mL |
| Lean ground beef | 1 lb. | 454 g |
| Chopped carrot | 1 cup | 250 mL |
| Chopped celery | 1 cup | 250 mL |
| Chopped onion | 1 cup | 250 mL |
| Chopped red pepper | 1 cup | 250 mL |
| Garlic cloves, minced | 2 | 2 |
| (or 1/2 tsp., 2 mL, powder) | | |
| All-purpose flour | 1 tbsp. | 15 mL |
| Ground ginger | 1/2 tsp. | 2 mL |
| Pepper | 1/4 tsp. | 1 mL |
| Prepared beef broth | 1 cup | 250 mL |
| Thick teriyaki basting sauce | 1/3 cup | 75 mL |

Combine water and salt in large saucepan. Bring to a boil. Add pasta. Boil, uncovered, for 12 to 14 minutes, stirring occasionally, until tender but firm. Drain. Return to same pot. Cover to keep warm.

Heat cooking oil in large frying pan on medium-high. Add next 6 ingredients. Cook for about 10 minutes, stirring frequently, until beef is no longer pink.

Add next 3 ingredients. Heat and stir for 2 minutes.

Add broth and teriyaki sauce. Heat and stir until boiling and thickened. Add pasta. Stir to coat. Makes about 9 cups (2.25 L).

*1 cup (250 mL): 219 Calories; 6.7 g Total Fat (2.8 g Mono, 0.5 g Poly, 2.2 g Sat); 33 mg Cholesterol; 25 g Carbohydrate; 2 g Fibre; 14 g Protein; 446 mg Sodium*

# Spicy Sausage Ratatouille

*Sure, vegetables are nice, but sometimes you're in the mood for something meaty and magnificent! We've added spicy sausage to this classic veggie dish for those times when nothing else will do.*

| | | |
|---|---|---|
| Water | 12 cups | 3 L |
| Salt | 1 1/2 tsp. | 7 mL |
| Whole-wheat penne pasta | 3 cups | 750 mL |
| Hot Italian sausage | 3/4 lb. | 340 g |
| Olive (or cooking) oil | 1 tbsp. | 15 mL |
| Chopped red onion | 1 cup | 250 mL |
| Chopped peeled eggplant (3/4 inch, 2 cm, pieces) | 3 cups | 750 mL |
| Chopped zucchini (with peel), 3/4 inch (2 cm) pieces | 2 cups | 500 mL |
| Chopped red pepper | 1 cup | 250 mL |
| Chili powder | 2 tsp. | 10 mL |
| Garlic powder | 1/2 tsp. | 2 mL |
| Salt | 1/2 tsp. | 2 mL |
| Pepper | 1/4 tsp. | 1 mL |
| Can of diced tomatoes (with juice) | 19 oz. | 540 mL |
| Can of tomato sauce | 14 oz. | 398 mL |
| Grated Italian cheese blend | 1 1/2 cups | 375 mL |

Combine water and salt in Dutch oven. Bring to a boil. Add pasta. Boil, uncovered, for 5 minutes, stirring occasionally. Drain. Transfer to greased 9 x 13 inch (22 x 33 cm) baking dish.

Heat large frying pan on medium. Add sausage. Cook for about 10 minutes, turning several times, until browned on all sides. Remove to paper towel-lined plate to drain. Let stand for 10 minutes. Cut into 1/4 inch (6 mm) slices. Add to pasta.

*(continued on next page)*

Heat olive oil in same frying pan on medium. Add onion. Cook for about 5 minutes, stirring occasionally, until softened.

Add next 7 ingredients. Cook for about 10 minutes, stirring occasionally, until eggplant is softened.

Add tomatoes with juice and tomato sauce. Stir. Add to pasta mixture. Toss. Sprinkle with cheese. Cover with greased foil. Bake in 350°F (175°C) oven for about 45 minutes until bubbling and cheese is melted. Serves 6.

*1 serving: 501 Calories; 19.1 g Total Fat (5.1 g Mono, 1.4 g Poly, 7.3 g Sat); 36 mg Cholesterol; 62 g Carbohydrate; 7 g Fibre; 24 g Protein; 1328 mg Sodium*

Pictured on page 35.

---

### Paré Pointer

*Fleas travel from dog to dog by itch hiking.*

# Beef Satay Linguine

*The classic beef skewer loses the stick and gains a hearty helping of pasta and tender-crisp veggies. We think this trade-off's more than fair!*

| | | |
|---|---|---|
| Frozen concentrated orange juice, thawed | 1/2 cup | 125 mL |
| Peanut sauce | 3 tbsp. | 50 mL |
| Rice vinegar | 3 tbsp. | 50 mL |
| Brown sugar, packed | 1 tbsp. | 15 mL |
| Soy sauce | 1 tbsp. | 15 mL |
| Ground ginger | 1 tsp. | 5 mL |
| Garlic powder | 1/2 tsp. | 2 mL |
| Pepper | 1/2 tsp. | 2 mL |
| Beef top sirloin steak | 1 lb. | 454 g |
| Water | 12 cups | 3 L |
| Salt | 1 1/2 tsp. | 7 mL |
| Linguine | 10 oz. | 285 g |
| Cooking oil | 2 tsp. | 10 mL |
| Cooking oil | 1 tsp. | 5 mL |
| Thinly sliced onion | 1 cup | 250 mL |
| Thinly sliced red pepper | 1 1/2 cups | 375 mL |
| Thinly sliced yellow pepper | 1 1/2 cups | 375 mL |

Combine first 8 ingredients in medium bowl. Cut steak across the grain into thin strips. Add to bowl. Toss to coat. Let stand for 10 minutes. Remove beef from marinade with slotted spoon. Reserve marinade.

Bring water and salt to a boil in Dutch oven. Add pasta. Boil, uncovered, for 9 to 11 minutes, stirring occasionally, until tender but firm. Drain. Return to same pot. Cover to keep warm.

Heat first amount of cooking oil in large frying pan on medium-high. Add beef. Cook for 3 to 5 minutes, stirring occasionally, until no longer pink. Transfer beef and liquids to small bowl. Cover to keep warm. Reduce heat to medium.

Heat second amount of cooking oil in same pan. Add onion. Cook for 5 to 10 minutes, stirring often, until onion is softened. Add reserved marinade. Bring to a boil.

Add red and yellow pepper. Cook for 3 to 5 minutes, stirring occasionally, until pepper is almost tender-crisp. Add pasta, beef and juices. Heat and stir for 1 to 2 minutes until coated and heated through. Makes about 8 cups (2 L).

*(continued on next page)*

Beef & Pork

*1 cup (250 mL):* 308 Calories; 8.0 g Total Fat (3.4 g Mono, 1.1 g Poly, 2.0 g Sat); 30 mg Cholesterol; 40 g Carbohydrate; 2 g Fibre; 19 g Protein; 209 mg Sodium

Pictured on page 35.

# Homey Mac And Cheese Bake

*Always a family favourite, this hearty mac and cheese is dressed up with ham, Parmesan and cayenne spice. A great way to use up leftover ham.*

| | | |
|---|---|---|
| Slices of white (or whole-wheat) bread, crusts removed, processed into crumbs | 3 | 3 |
| Grated Parmesan cheese | 2 tbsp. | 30 mL |
| Butter (or hard margarine), melted | 1 tbsp. | 15 mL |
| Paprika | 1/2 tsp. | 2 mL |
| Water | 12 cups | 3 L |
| Salt | 1 1/2 tsp. | 7 mL |
| Elbow macaroni | 2 1/2 cups | 625 mL |
| Butter (or hard margarine) | 2 tbsp. | 30 mL |
| All-purpose flour | 2 tbsp. | 30 mL |
| Milk | 3 cups | 750 mL |
| Diced cooked ham | 1 1/2 cups | 375 mL |
| Grated mozzarella cheese | 1 cup | 250 mL |
| Grated sharp Cheddar cheese | 1 cup | 250 mL |
| Cayenne pepper | 1/4 tsp. | 1 mL |

Combine first 4 ingredients in small bowl. Set aside.

Combine water and salt in Dutch oven. Bring to a boil. Add pasta. Boil, uncovered, for 8 to 10 minutes, stirring occasionally, until tender but firm. Drain. Return to same pot.

Melt second amount of butter in large saucepan on medium. Add flour. Heat and stir for 1 minute. Slowly add milk, stirring constantly, until boiling and thickened.

Add remaining 4 ingredients and pasta. Heat and stir until cheese is melted. Transfer to greased 2 quart (2 L) casserole. Sprinkle with crumb mixture. Bake, uncovered, in 375°F (190°C) oven for about 30 minutes until golden and bubbly. Serves 6.

*1 serving:* 519 Calories; 22 g Total Fat (6.4 g Mono, 1.1 g Poly, 11.7 g Sat); 80 mg Cholesterol; 48 g Carbohydrate; 2 g Fibre; 31 g Protein; 473 mg Sodium

# Pesto Olive Lasagna

*If you love olives, you'll go crazy over this creative combination of pasta, pesto, sausage and cheese.*

| | | |
|---|---|---|
| Cooking oil | 2 tsp. | 10 mL |
| Lean ground beef | 1 lb. | 454 g |
| Hot Italian sausage, casing removed | 1/2 lb. | 225 g |
| Chopped onion | 1 cup | 250 mL |
| Garlic cloves, minced (or 1/2 tsp., 2 mL, powder) | 2 | 2 |
| Sliced fresh white mushrooms | 2 cups | 500 mL |
| Can of diced tomatoes (with juice) | 28 oz. | 796 mL |
| Prepared beef broth | 1 cup | 250 mL |
| Can of tomato paste | 5 1/2 oz. | 156 mL |
| Dried basil | 1 tsp. | 5 mL |
| Bay leaves (see Note) | 2 | 2 |
| Ricotta cheese | 2 cups | 500 mL |
| Jar of sun-dried tomato pesto | 9 1/2 oz. | 270 mL |
| Can of sliced black olives, drained | 4 1/2 oz. | 125 mL |
| Oven-ready lasagna noodles | 9 | 9 |
| Grated mozzarella cheese | 2 cups | 500 mL |
| Grated Parmesan cheese | 1/2 cup | 125 mL |

Heat cooking oil in Dutch oven on medium-high. Add next 4 ingredients. Scramble-fry for about 10 minutes until no longer pink. Drain.

Add mushrooms. Cook, uncovered, for 2 to 4 minutes, stirring occasionally, until mushrooms start to soften.

Add next 5 ingredients. Stir. Bring to a boil. Reduce heat to medium-low. Simmer, covered, for about 30 minutes, stirring occasionally, to blend flavours. Discard bay leaves. Remove from heat.

Combine ricotta and pesto in medium bowl. Add olives. Stir.

*(continued on next page)*

To assemble, layer ingredients in greased 9 x 13 inch (22 x 33 cm) baking dish as follows:

1. 1 cup (250 mL) meat sauce
2. 3 noodles
3. Half of remaining meat sauce
4. 3 noodles
5. Half of pesto mixture
6. Remaining meat sauce
7. Remaining 3 noodles
8. Remaining pesto mixture

Sprinkle with mozzarella and Parmesan cheese. Cover with greased foil. Bake in 350°F (175°C) oven for about 50 minutes until noodles are softened. Remove foil. Broil on centre rack in oven for 5 minutes until cheese is golden. Cuts into 8 pieces.

*1 piece: 506 Calories; 23.2 g Total Fat (6.2 g Mono, 1.2 g Poly, 10.7 g Sat); 80 mg Cholesterol; 35 g Carbohydrate; 3 g Fibre; 38 g Protein; 1549 mg Sodium*

Pictured on page 36.

**Note:** While stirring, be careful not to break up the bay leaves.

---

### Paré Pointer

*Children are a comfort in your old age—and they sure help you reach it sooner.*

# Cannelloni Olé

*Cannelloni shells can hold more than just cheese! Here we've filled them with beef and beans for an unexpected Mexican twist on this Italian favourite.*

| | | |
|---|---|---|
| Can of refried beans | 14 oz. | 398 mL |
| Salsa | 2 tbsp. | 30 mL |
| Yellow cornmeal | 2 tbsp. | 30 mL |
| Chili powder | 1/2 tsp. | 2 mL |
| Ground cumin | 1/4 tsp. | 1 mL |
| Lean ground beef | 1/2 lb. | 225 g |
| Cooking oil | 1 tsp. | 5 mL |
| Chopped onion | 1/2 cup | 125 mL |
| Garlic clove, minced | 1 | 1 |
| (or 1/4 tsp., 1 mL, powder) | | |
| Can of diced tomatoes (with juice) | 14 oz. | 398 mL |
| Salsa | 1 1/2 cups | 375 mL |
| Water | 1/2 cup | 125 mL |
| Granulated sugar | 1 tsp. | 5 mL |
| Salt | 1/2 tsp. | 2 mL |
| Pepper | 1/2 tsp. | 2 mL |
| Oven-ready cannelloni shells | 12 | 12 |
| Grated jalapeño Monterey Jack cheese | 1 cup | 250 mL |

Combine 2/3 cup (150 mL) refried beans and next 4 ingredients in large bowl, reserving remaining beans. Add beef to bean mixture. Mix well. Set aside.

Heat cooking oil in medium frying pan on medium. Add onion. Cook for about 5 minutes, stirring often, until softened. Add garlic. Heat and stir for 1 to 2 minutes until fragrant.

Add next 6 ingredients and reserved refried beans. Stir. Bring to a boil. Spread half of sauce in greased 9 x 13 inch (22 x 33 cm) baking dish.

Fill cannelloni shells with beef mixture. Arrange in single layer over sauce in baking dish. Pour remaining sauce over filled shells. Bake, covered, in 350°F (175°C) oven for about 45 minutes until pasta is tender and internal temperature reaches 160°F (70°C). Sprinkle with cheese. Bake, uncovered, for about 5 minutes until cheese is bubbling. Makes 12 cannelloni.

*1 cannelloni: 161 Calories; 5.8 g Total Fat (1.1 g Mono, 0.2 g Poly, 2.5 g Sat); 21 mg Cholesterol; 18 g Carbohydrate; 2 g Fibre; 9 g Protein; 570 mg Sodium*

# One-Pot Beef Fettuccine

*Think a one-pot pasta dish is impossible? Not if you cook the pasta and sauce together!*

| | | |
|---|---|---|
| Bacon slices, chopped | 5 | 5 |
| Beef top sirloin steak, cut into 1/2 inch (12 mm) cubes | 1 lb. | 454 g |
| Diced carrot | 1 cup | 250 mL |
| Diced onion | 1 cup | 250 mL |
| Diced celery | 3/4 cup | 175 mL |
| Prepared beef broth | 2 cups | 500 mL |
| Can of tomato sauce | 14 oz. | 398 mL |
| Water | 1 cup | 250 mL |
| Dry (or alcohol-free) red wine | 1/2 cup | 125 mL |
| Tomato paste (see Tip, page 121) | 2 tbsp. | 30 mL |
| Garlic clove, minced (or 1/4 tsp., 1 mL, powder) | 1 | 1 |
| Pepper | 1/4 tsp. | 1 mL |
| Fettuccine, broken in half | 8 oz. | 225 g |
| Grated Parmesan cheese | 1/4 cup | 60 mL |

Cook bacon in Dutch oven on medium-high until crisp. Transfer with slotted spoon to paper towel-lined plate to drain. Drain and discard all but 1 tbsp. (15 mL) drippings.

Add beef to same pot. Cook, uncovered, for 2 to 4 minutes, stirring occasionally, until browned. Reduce heat to medium.

Add next 3 ingredients. Stir. Cook, uncovered, for about 5 minutes, stirring occasionally, until vegetables are softened.

Add next 7 ingredients. Stir, scraping any brown bits from bottom of pan. Bring to a boil. Reduce heat to medium-low. Simmer, covered, for about 30 minutes until beef is tender.

Add pasta and bacon. Stir. Simmer, covered, for about 20 minutes, stirring often, until pasta is tender but firm.

Sprinkle with cheese. Makes about 6 1/2 cups (1.6 L).

*1 cup (250 mL): 369 Calories; 11.3 g Total Fat (3.9 g Mono, 0.7 g Poly, 4.4 g Sat); 49 mg Cholesterol; 37 g Carbohydrate; 3 g Fibre; 25 g Protein; 1014 mg Sodium*

# Bacon Feta Carbonara

*The smoky flavour of bacon pairs perfectly with a rich cheese sauce.*

| | | |
|---|---|---|
| Water | 12 cups | 3 L |
| Salt | 1 1/2 tsp. | 7 mL |
| Spaghettini | 12 oz. | 340 g |
| Whipping cream | 1/2 cup | 125 mL |
| Egg yolks (large) | 2 | 2 |
| Olive (or cooking) oil | 1 tsp. | 5 mL |
| Bacon slices, diced | 4 | 4 |
| Garlic clove, minced | 1 | 1 |
| (or 1/4 tsp., 1 mL, powder) | | |
| Ground nutmeg | 1/8 tsp. | 0.5 mL |
| Pepper | 1/8 tsp. | 0.5 mL |
| Crumbled feta cheese | 3/4 cup | 175 mL |
| Grated Parmesan cheese | 1/4 cup | 60 mL |

Combine water and salt in Dutch oven. Bring to a boil. Add pasta. Boil, uncovered, for 9 to 11 minutes, stirring occasionally, until tender but firm. Drain, reserving 1/2 cup (125 mL) cooking water. Return to same pot.

Meanwhile, whisk cream and egg yolks in small bowl until combined. Set aside.

Heat olive oil in large frying pan on medium. Add bacon. Cook, stirring occasionally, until crisp.

Add next 3 ingredients. Heat and stir for 1 minute. Reduce heat to medium-low. Add pasta. Toss to coat. Add reserved cooking water to cream mixture. Stir. Add to frying pan. Toss to coat.

Add feta and Parmesan cheese. Toss. Serve immediately. Makes about 6 cups (1.5 L).

*1 cup (250 mL): 412 Calories; 20.1 g Total Fat (6.4 g Mono, 1.4 g Poly, 9.7 g Sat); 115 mg Cholesterol; 44 g Carbohydrate; trace Fibre; 15 g Protein; 464 mg Sodium*

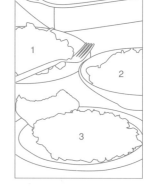

1. Chili Chicken Pasta, page 61
2. Red Curry Chicken Rotini, page 64
3. Bruschetta Chicken, page 67

Props courtesy of: Mikasa Home Store
Totally Bamboo
Pyrex® Storage
Wiltshire®

Beef & Pork

# Lemon Tahini Chicken

*The nutty flavour of sesame paste and fresh lemon pair with tender chicken and pasta for a truly divine combination.*

| | | |
|---|---|---|
| Water | 12 cups | 3 L |
| Salt | 1 1/2 tsp. | 7 mL |
| Radiatore pasta | 4 cups | 1 L |
| Cooking oil | 2 tsp. | 10 mL |
| Boneless, skinless chicken thighs, cut into 1 inch (2.5 cm) pieces | 3/4 lb. | 340 g |
| Garlic cloves, minced (or 3/4 tsp., 4 mL, powder) | 3 | 3 |
| Chopped roasted red pepper | 1/2 cup | 125 mL |
| Tahini (sesame paste) | 1/2 cup | 125 mL |
| Lemon juice | 3 tbsp. | 50 mL |
| Grated lemon zest | 1 tsp. | 5 mL |
| Salt | 1 tsp. | 5 mL |
| Pepper | 1/2 tsp. | 2 mL |
| Chopped fresh parsley | 1/4 cup | 60 mL |

Combine water and salt in Dutch oven. Bring to a boil. Add pasta. Boil, uncovered, for 7 to 9 minutes, stirring occasionally, until tender but firm. Drain, reserving 1 1/4 cups (300 mL) cooking water. Return pasta to same pot. Cover to keep warm.

Heat cooking oil in medium frying pan on medium. Add chicken. Cook for 5 to 10 minutes, stirring occasionally, until chicken is starting to brown. Add garlic. Heat and stir for 1 minute until fragrant.

Add next 6 ingredients and reserved cooking water. Stir. Cook for about 5 minutes, stirring occasionally, until chicken is no longer pink inside and sauce is slightly thickened. Add to pasta.

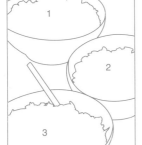

Add parsley. Stir. Makes about 7 cups (1.75 L). Serve immediately.

*1 cup (250 mL): 346 Calories; 14.7 g Total Fat (5.6 g Mono, 5.2 g Poly, 2.4 g Sat); 32 mg Cholesterol; 35 g Carbohydrate; 2 g Fibre; 17 g Protein; 578 mg Sodium*

1. Spaghetti Chicken Stir-Fry, page 62
2. Bourbon Chicken Pilaf, page 68
3. Asian Chicken Supreme, page 70

# Turkey Pasta Pie

*Like quiche? It's even better when you substitute the heavy crust with tender macaroni.*

| | | |
|---|---|---|
| Water | 8 cups | 2 L |
| Salt | 1 tsp. | 5 mL |
| Elbow macaroni | 1 cup | 250 mL |
| | | |
| Cooking oil | 2 tsp. | 10 mL |
| Ground turkey | 3/4 lb. | 340 g |
| Chopped onion | 1 cup | 250 mL |
| Garlic cloves, minced | 2 | 2 |
| (or 1/2 tsp., 2 mL, powder) | | |
| | | |
| Broccoli florets | 1 cup | 250 mL |
| Seasoned salt | 1/2 tsp. | 2 mL |
| Dried rosemary, crushed | 1/4 tsp. | 1 mL |
| Ground sage | 1/4 tsp. | 1 mL |
| Pepper | 1/4 tsp. | 1 mL |
| | | |
| Large eggs, fork-beaten | 4 | 4 |
| Milk | 1 1/2 cups | 375 mL |
| Grated sharp Cheddar cheese | 1 cup | 250 mL |
| All-purpose flour | 1/4 cup | 60 mL |
| Real bacon bits | 2 tbsp. | 30 mL |
| | | |
| Grated sharp Cheddar cheese | 1/2 cup | 125 mL |

Bring water and salt to a boil in large saucepan. Add pasta. Boil, uncovered, for 8 to 10 minutes, stirring occasionally, until tender but firm. Drain.

Heat cooking oil in large frying pan on medium. Add next 3 ingredients. Scramble-fry for about 10 minutes until turkey is no longer pink.

Add next 5 ingredients. Cook for about 3 minutes until broccoli starts to soften. Remove from heat.

Whisk eggs and milk in large bowl. Add next 3 ingredients and pasta. Stir. Add turkey mixture. Stir. Transfer to greased 2 quart (2 L) casserole.

Sprinkle with second amount of cheese. Bake, covered, in 350°F (175°C) oven for 30 minutes. Bake, uncovered, for another 15 to 20 minutes until knife inserted in centre comes out clean. Let stand for 10 minutes. Serves 4.

*1 serving: 583 Calories; 28.3 g Total Fat (6.0 g Mono, 1.2 g Poly, 12.9 g Sat); 316 mg Cholesterol; 39 g Carbohydrate; 2 g Fibre; 43 g Protein; 730 mg Sodium*

# Lemon Chicken Pasta Toss

*A pasta dish without sauce doesn't have to be plain-Jane. With flavourful chicken, tangy lemon and herbs, you won't miss the sauce at all.*

| | | |
|---|---|---|
| All-purpose flour | 2 tbsp. | 30 mL |
| Poultry seasoning | 3/4 tsp. | 4 mL |
| Boneless, skinless chicken breast halves, cut into 1/4 inch (6 mm) strips | 1 lb. | 454 g |
| Butter (or hard margarine) | 1 tbsp. | 15 mL |
| Olive (or cooking) oil | 1 tbsp. | 15 mL |
| Garlic cloves, minced (or 1/2 tsp., 2 mL, powder) | 2 | 2 |
| Prepared chicken broth | 1/4 cup | 60 mL |
| Lemon juice | 1 tbsp. | 15 mL |
| Dried marjoram | 1 1/2 tsp. | 7 mL |
| Grated lemon zest | 1 tsp. | 5 mL |
| Salt | 1/2 tsp. | 2 mL |
| Pepper | 1/4 tsp. | 1 mL |
| Water | 12 cups | 3 L |
| Salt | 1 1/2 tsp. | 7 mL |
| Angel hair pasta | 8 oz. | 225 g |
| Chopped fresh parsley | 1/4 cup | 60 mL |

Combine flour and poultry seasoning in large resealable freezer bag. Add chicken. Toss to coat.

Heat butter and olive oil in large frying pan on medium. Add chicken. Cook for about 5 minutes, stirring occasionally, until no longer pink. Reduce heat to medium-low.

Add garlic. Cook and stir for about 2 minutes until garlic is fragrant and softened. Add next 6 ingredients. Stir. Bring to a boil. Remove from heat. Cover to keep warm.

Combine water and salt in Dutch oven. Bring to a boil. Add pasta. Boil, uncovered, for 3 to 5 minutes, stirring occasionally, until tender but firm. Drain, reserving 1/4 cup (60 mL) cooking water. Return to same pot.

Add parsley, chicken mixture and reserved cooking water to pasta. Toss. Makes about 6 cups (1.5 L).

*1 cup (250 mL): 273 Calories; 5.9 g Total Fat (2.4 g Mono, 0.6 g Poly, 1.8 g Sat); 49 mg Cholesterol; 30 g Carbohydrate; 1 g Fibre; 23 g Protein; 297 mg Sodium*

# Turkey Meatball Bake

*It may look like rice, but it's not! Orzo is actually pasta shaped like tiny grains of rice. Turkey meatballs add a hearty touch to this creamy, cheesy dish.*

| | | |
|---|---|---|
| Large egg, fork-beaten | 1 | 1 |
| Fine dry bread crumbs | 1/4 cup | 60 mL |
| Grated lemon zest | 1/2 tsp. | 2 mL |
| Ground cinnamon | 1/4 tsp. | 1 mL |
| Ground nutmeg | 1/4 tsp. | 1 mL |
| Lean ground turkey | 1 lb. | 454 g |
| Cooking oil | 1 tbsp. | 15 mL |
| Butter (or hard margarine) | 2 tbsp. | 30 mL |
| Chopped onion | 1/2 cup | 125 mL |
| Garlic clove, minced | 1 | 1 |
| (or 1/4 tsp., 1 mL, powder) | | |
| All-purpose flour | 2 tbsp. | 30 mL |
| Prepared chicken broth | 1 1/2 cups | 375 mL |
| Milk | 1 cup | 250 mL |
| Soft goat (chèvre) cheese | 1/4 cup | 60 mL |
| Orzo | 1 cup | 250 mL |
| Chopped fresh parsley | 2 tbsp. | 30 mL |

Combine first 5 ingredients in large bowl. Add turkey. Mix well. Roll into 1 inch (2.5 cm) balls. Makes about 34 turkey balls.

Heat cooking oil in large frying pan on medium-high. Add meatballs. Cook for 3 to 5 minutes, stirring often, until browned. Remove with slotted spoon to paper-towel lined plate. Cover to keep warm. Drain and discard drippings.

Melt butter in same large frying pan on medium. Add onion and garlic. Cook for about 5 minutes until onion is softened.

Add flour. Heat and stir for 1 minute. Slowly add broth and milk, stirring constantly, until mixture starts to boil and thicken. Add cheese. Heat and stir until melted. Add orzo. Stir. Transfer to greased 2 quart (2 L) casserole. Arrange meatballs on top. Bake, covered, in 400°F (205°C) oven for about 30 minutes until pasta is tender.

Sprinkle with parsley. Makes about 6 cups (1.5 L).

*1 cup (250 mL): 352 Calories; 15.0 g Total Fat (3.1 g Mono, 1.0 g Poly, 5.9 g Sat); 96 mg Cholesterol; 30 g Carbohydrate; 2 g Fibre; 24 g Protein; 555 mg Sodium*

# Blue Cheese Tortellini

*Feeling blue? This creamy sauce of earthy blue cheese and tender-crisp broccoli makes a hearty pairing for tortellini. True comfort food, this dish is sure to cheer you up in no time at all.*

| | | |
|---|---|---|
| Cooking oil | 2 tsp. | 10 mL |
| Boneless, skinless chicken breast halves, cut into bite-sized pieces | 1 lb. | 454 g |
| Chopped onion | 1 cup | 250 mL |
| Garlic clove, minced (or 1/4 tsp., 1 mL, powder) | 1 | 1 |
| All-purpose flour | 2 tbsp. | 30 mL |
| Homogenized milk | 2 cups | 500 mL |
| Prepared chicken broth | 1 cup | 250 mL |
| Crumbled blue cheese | 3 1/2 oz. | 100 g |
| Pepper | 1/4 tsp. | 1 mL |
| Water | 12 cups | 3 L |
| Salt | 1 1/2 tsp. | 7 mL |
| Package of fresh cheese tortellini | 12 1/2 oz. | 350 g |
| Broccoli florets | 2 cups | 500 mL |

Heat cooking oil in large frying pan on medium. Add chicken. Cook for 5 to 10 minutes, stirring occasionally, until browned. Remove with slotted spoon to large plate. Cover to keep warm.

Add onion and garlic to same frying pan. Cook for about 5 to 10 minutes, stirring often, until onion is softened.

Sprinkle with flour. Heat and stir for 1 minute. Slowly add milk and broth, stirring constantly, until smooth. Heat and stir for about 5 minutes until boiling and thickened. Reduce heat to medium-low. Add cheese, pepper and chicken. Stir until cheese is melted.

Combine water and salt in Dutch oven. Bring to a boil. Add pasta. Boil, uncovered, for 6 minutes, stirring occasionally. Add broccoli. Cook for about 2 minutes, stirring occasionally, until tortellini is tender but firm and broccoli is tender-crisp. Drain. Add to chicken mixture. Stir. Makes about 6 1/2 cups (1.6 L).

*1 cup (250 mL): 379 Calories; 13.3 g Total Fat (4.2 g Mono, 1.2 g Poly, 6.7 g Sat); 85 mg Cholesterol; 34 g Carbohydrate; 2 g Fibre; 30 g Protein; 716 mg Sodium*

# Balsamic Orange Chicken

*Tortellini and tender morsels of chicken dressed in a tangy citrus and balsamic sauce. Change it up by using rotini or fusilli instead of tortellini.*

| | | |
|---|---|---|
| Olive (or cooking) oil | 1 tbsp. | 15 mL |
| Chopped portobello mushroom | 3 cups | 750 mL |
| Chopped onion | 1 cup | 250 mL |
| Garlic cloves, minced | 2 | 2 |
| (or 1/2 tsp., 2 mL, powder) | | |
| Boneless, skinless chicken thighs, cut into bite-sized pieces | 1 lb. | 454 g |
| Orange juice | 1 cup | 250 mL |
| Balsamic vinegar | 2 tbsp. | 30 mL |
| Brown sugar, packed | 2 tsp. | 10 mL |
| Dijon mustard | 2 tsp. | 10 mL |
| Salt | 1/2 tsp. | 2 mL |
| Pepper | 1/4 tsp. | 1 mL |
| Water | 1 tbsp. | 15 mL |
| Cornstarch | 2 tsp. | 10 mL |
| Water | 12 cups | 3 L |
| Salt | 1 1/2 tsp. | 7 mL |
| Package of fresh cheese tortellini | 12 oz. | 350 g |
| Grated Parmesan cheese | 2 tbsp. | 30 mL |
| Chopped fresh basil | 1 tbsp. | 15 mL |

Heat olive oil in large frying pan on medium. Add next 3 ingredients. Cook for 5 to 10 minutes, stirring often, until onion is softened and liquid has evaporated.

Add chicken. Cook for about 10 minutes, stirring occasionally, until chicken is no longer pink.

Add next 6 ingredients. Stir. Bring to a boil. Cook, covered, for about 5 minutes to blend flavours.

Stir water into cornstarch in small cup. Add to chicken mixture. Heat and stir for 1 to 2 minutes until bubbling and thickened.

Combine water and salt in Dutch oven. Bring to a boil. Add pasta. Boil, uncovered, for 8 to 11 minutes, stirring occasionally, until tender but firm. Drain. Add to chicken mixture. Stir gently to coat. Transfer to serving dish.

*(continued on next page)*

Sprinkle with cheese and basil. Makes about 6 1/2 cups (1.6 L).

*1 cup (250 mL): 340 Calories; 12.1 g Total Fat (4.6 g Mono, 1.8 g Poly, 4.1 g Sat);*
*70 mg Cholesterol; 36 g Carbohydrate; 2 g Fibre; 22 g Protein; 466 mg Sodium*

# Chili Chicken Pasta

*Like chili? Like pasta? After you try this clever one-pot dish, you'll wonder*
*why you've never combined them before.*

| | | |
|---|---|---|
| Cooking oil | 2 tsp. | 10 mL |
| Lean ground chicken | 1 lb. | 454 g |
| Chopped onion | 1 cup | 250 mL |
| Garlic cloves, minced | 2 | 2 |
| (or 1/2 tsp., 2 mL, powder) | | |
| Can of diced tomatoes (with juice) | 28 oz. | 796 mL |
| Can of kidney beans, rinsed and drained | 19 oz. | 540 mL |
| Prepared chicken broth | 1 cup | 250 mL |
| Water | 1 cup | 250 mL |
| Tomato paste (see Tip, page 121) | 1 tbsp. | 15 mL |
| Chili powder | 2 tsp. | 10 mL |
| Chopped pickled jalapeño pepper slices | 2 tsp. | 10 mL |
| Granulated sugar | 1/2 tsp. | 2 mL |
| Salt | 1/4 tsp. | 1 mL |
| Pepper | 1/4 tsp. | 1 mL |
| Cavatappi pasta | 2 cups | 500 mL |
| Grated jalapeño Monterey Jack cheese | 1 cup | 250 mL |

Heat cooking oil in Dutch oven on medium. Add next 3 ingredients. Cook, uncovered, for about 10 minutes, stirring occasionally, until chicken is no longer pink.

Add next 10 ingredients. Stir. Bring to a boil.

Add pasta. Stir. Cook, covered, on medium-low for about 20 minutes, stirring occasionally, until pasta is tender but firm. Remove from heat. Let stand, covered, for 10 minutes.

Sprinkle with cheese. Makes about 9 2/3 cups (2.4 L).

*1 cup (250 mL): 249 Calories; 9.0 g Total Fat (0.7 g Mono, 0.5 g Poly, 3.3 g Sat); 41 mg Cholesterol;*
*27 g Carbohydrate; 3 g Fibre; 16 g Protein; 614 mg Sodium*

Pictured on page 53.

# Spaghetti Chicken Stir-Fry

*Who needs chow mein noodles when spaghetti makes the perfect partner for
these crisp and saucy stir-fried veggies. A simple and healthy entree.*

| | | |
|---|---|---|
| Water | 8 cups | 2 L |
| Salt | 1 tsp. | 5 mL |
| Spaghetti, broken into thirds | 6 oz. | 170 g |
| Cooking oil | 2 tsp. | 10 mL |
| Boneless, skinless chicken breast halves, thinly sliced | 3/4 lb. | 340 g |
| Sliced carrot | 1 cup | 250 mL |
| Sliced onion | 1 cup | 250 mL |
| Finely grated gingerroot | 2 tsp. | 10 mL |
| Garlic clove, minced (or 1/4 tsp., 1 mL, powder) | 1 | 1 |
| Can of cut baby corn, drained | 14 oz. | 398 mL |
| Chopped fresh asparagus (1 inch, 2.5 cm, pieces) | 1 cup | 250 mL |
| Small broccoli florets | 1 cup | 250 mL |
| Fresh bean sprouts | 1 cup | 250 mL |
| Sliced green onion | 1/2 cup | 125 mL |
| Prepared chicken broth | 1/4 cup | 60 mL |
| Soy sauce | 2 tbsp. | 30 mL |
| Sesame oil (for flavour) | 2 tsp. | 10 mL |

Combine water and salt in large saucepan. Bring to a boil. Add pasta. Boil,
uncovered, for 10 to 12 minutes, stirring occasionally, until tender but firm.
Drain. Return to same pot.

Heat large frying pan or wok on medium-high until very hot. Add cooking
oil. Add chicken. Stir-fry for about 3 minutes until no longer pink. Transfer
to medium bowl. Cover to keep warm.

Reduce heat to medium. Add next 4 ingredients to same frying pan.
Stir-fry for 2 minutes.

Add next 3 ingredients. Stir-fry for about 3 minutes until vegetables are
tender-crisp.

Add remaining 5 ingredients, chicken and pasta. Stir-fry for 1 to 2 minutes
until combined and heated through. Makes about 9 cups (2.25 L).

*(continued on next page)*

Chicken & Turkey

*1 cup (250 mL): 209 Calories; 3.6 g Total Fat (0.9 g Mono, 0.8 g Poly, 0.5 g Sat); 22 mg Cholesterol; 32 g Carbohydrate; 3 g Fibre; 15 g Protein; 379 mg Sodium*

Pictured on page 54.

# Spicy Chicken Spaghetti

*The richness of this cheesy sauce is countered by the heat of jalapeño peppers.*

| | | |
|---|---|---|
| Water | 8 cups | 2 L |
| Salt | 1 tsp. | 5 mL |
| Whole-wheat spaghetti, broken into 4 pieces | 8 oz. | 225 g |
| Olive (or cooking) oil | 1 tbsp. | 15 mL |
| Boneless, skinless chicken breast halves, cut into 1/2 inch (12 mm) cubes | 3/4 lb. | 340 g |
| Sliced fresh white mushrooms | 3 cups | 750 mL |
| Can of condensed cream of mushroom soup | 10 oz. | 284 mL |
| Milk | 1/3 cup | 75 mL |
| Can of diced tomatoes (with juice) | 14 oz. | 398 mL |
| Finely chopped pickled jalapeño peppers | 1 tbsp. | 15 mL |
| Dried basil | 1 1/2 tsp. | 7 mL |
| Pepper | 1/2 tsp. | 2 mL |
| Garlic powder | 1/4 tsp. | 1 mL |
| Grated jalapeño Monterey Jack cheese | 1 cup | 250 mL |

Combine water and salt in large saucepan. Bring to a boil. Add pasta. Boil, uncovered, for 10 to 12 minutes, stirring occasionally, until tender but firm. Drain. Return to same pot. Cover to keep warm.

Heat olive oil in large frying pan on medium. Add chicken. Cook for about 5 minutes, stirring occasionally, until no longer pink.

Add mushrooms. Cook for 5 to 10 minutes, stirring occasionally, until liquid has evaporated and mushrooms are starting to brown. Add to pasta. Toss. Cover to keep warm.

Stir soup and milk in same frying pan until smooth. Add next 5 ingredients. Heat and stir on medium for 2 to 4 minutes until boiling.

Add cheese. Stir for about 30 seconds until melted. Add to pasta mixture. Toss to combine. Makes about 7 cups (1.75 L).

*1 cup (250 mL): 302 Calories; 10.8 g Total Fat (1.6 g Mono, 0.4 g Poly, 4.0 g Sat); 45 mg Cholesterol; 32 g Carbohydrate; 3 g Fibre; 21 g Protein; 608 mg Sodium*

# Red Curry Chicken Rotini

*You can almost taste the tropical sunshine in this bright and fruity curry dish with hearty chicken, creamy coconut, sweet apple and mango.*

| | | |
|---|---|---|
| Water | 12 cups | 3 L |
| Salt | 1 1/2 tsp. | 7 mL |
| Rotini pasta | 4 cups | 1 L |
| Cooking oil | 1 tbsp. | 15 mL |
| Boneless, skinless chicken thighs, cut into 1 inch (2.5 cm) pieces | 1 lb. | 454 g |
| Diced peeled tart apple (such as Granny Smith) | 1 1/2 cups | 375 mL |
| Chopped frozen mango, thawed | 1 cup | 250 mL |
| Thinly sliced onion | 1 cup | 250 mL |
| Thinly sliced red pepper | 1 cup | 250 mL |
| Garlic clove, minced (or 1/4 tsp., 1 mL, powder) | 1 | 1 |
| Can of coconut milk | 14 oz. | 398 mL |
| Prepared chicken broth | 1 cup | 250 mL |
| Fish sauce | 2 tbsp. | 30 mL |
| Sweet chili sauce | 2 tbsp. | 30 mL |
| Red curry paste | 1 tsp. | 5 mL |
| Lime juice | 1 tbsp. | 15 mL |
| Chopped fresh basil | 1 tbsp. | 15 mL |

Combine water and salt in Dutch oven. Bring to a boil. Add pasta. Boil, uncovered, for 12 to 14 minutes, stirring occasionally, until tender but firm. Drain. Return to same pot. Cover to keep warm.

Heat cooking oil in large frying pan on medium-high. Add chicken. Cook for 5 to 8 minutes, stirring occasionally, until starting to brown. Drain all but 1 tbsp. (15 mL) drippings.

Add next 5 ingredients. Reduce heat to medium. Cook for 5 to 10 minutes, stirring occasionally, until onion and apple are softened.

Add next 5 ingredients. Stir. Bring to a boil. Simmer, uncovered, for about 10 minutes until sauce is slightly thickened.

Add lime juice. Stir. Add to pasta. Toss. Transfer to serving bowl.

*(continued on next page)*

Chicken & Turkey

Sprinkle with basil. Makes about 8 cups (2 L).

*1 cup (250 mL): 367 Calories; 17.6 g Total Fat (3.1 g Mono, 1.7 g Poly, 10.8 g Sat); 37 mg Cholesterol; 37 g Carbohydrate; 3 g Fibre; 16 g Protein; 564 mg Sodium*

Pictured on page 53.

---

# Smoky Chicken Penne

*Smokin'! This spicy chicken penne has a double-dose of smoky flavour from bacon and chipotle peppers.*

| | | |
|---|---|---|
| Bacon slices, diced | 4 | 4 |
| Lean ground chicken | 1 lb. | 454 g |
| Chopped onion | 1/2 cup | 125 mL |
| Garlic clove, minced | 1 | 1 |
| (or 1/4 tsp., 1 mL, powder) | | |
| Italian seasoning | 1 tsp. | 5 mL |
| Pasta sauce | 4 cups | 1 L |
| Penne pasta | 4 cups | 1 L |
| Water | 4 cups | 1 L |
| Finely chopped chipotle peppers in adobo sauce (see Tip, page 116) | 1/2 tsp. | 2 mL |
| Diced green pepper | 1 cup | 250 mL |
| Grated mozzarella cheese (optional) | 1/2 cup | 125 mL |

Cook bacon in Dutch oven on medium-high, stirring occasionally, until starting to crisp. Add chicken. Scramble-fry for about 5 minutes until chicken is no longer pink.

Add next 3 ingredients. Stir. Cook, uncovered, for about 3 minutes, stirring occasionally, until onion starts to soften.

Add next 4 ingredients. Stir. Bring to a boil, stirring often. Reduce heat to medium-low. Simmer, covered, for about 15 minutes, stirring often, until pasta is almost tender.

Add green pepper. Stir. Cook, covered, for about 5 minutes until pasta is tender but firm and pepper is tender-crisp.

Sprinkle with cheese. Makes about 9 1/2 cups (2.4 L).

*1 cup (250 mL): 336 Calories; 9.4 g Total Fat (1.9 g Mono, 0.5 g Poly, 2.5 g Sat); 38 mg Cholesterol; 48 g Carbohydrate; 2 g Fibre; 17 g Protein; 378 mg Sodium*

Pictured on front cover.

# Mediterranean Tortellini

*This cheesy, colourful combination has all the warmth and flavour of a sunny Mediterranean day. Use spinach tortellini for colour contrast.*

| | | |
|---|---|---|
| Water | 12 cups | 3 L |
| Salt | 1 1/2 tsp. | 7 mL |
| Package of fresh cheese tortellini | 12 1/2 oz. | 350 g |
| Can of artichoke hearts, drained and quartered | 14 oz. | 398 mL |
| Sun-dried tomatoes in oil, drained and chopped | 1/4 cup | 60 mL |
| Butter (or hard margarine) | 2 tbsp. | 30 mL |
| Chopped onion | 1 cup | 250 mL |
| Garlic cloves, minced (or 1/2 tsp., 2 mL, powder) | 2 | 2 |
| All-purpose flour | 2 tbsp. | 30 mL |
| Milk | 2 1/4 cups | 550 mL |
| Chopped cooked chicken (see Note) | 2 cups | 500 mL |
| Pepper | 1/4 tsp. | 1 mL |
| Crumbled feta cheese | 1/2 cup | 125 mL |
| Chopped fresh basil | 1/4 cup | 60 mL |

Chopped fresh basil, for garnish

Combine water and salt in Dutch oven. Bring to a boil. Add pasta. Boil, uncovered, for 8 to 11 minutes, stirring occasionally, until tender but firm. Drain. Return to same pot.

Add artichoke and sun-dried tomato. Stir. Cover to keep warm.

Melt butter in large saucepan on medium. Add onion. Cook, uncovered, for 5 to 10 minutes, stirring often, until onion is softened. Add garlic. Heat and stir for about 1 minute until fragrant. Add flour. Heat and stir for 1 minute.

Slowly add milk, stirring constantly until smooth. Heat and stir for 5 to 8 minutes until boiling and thickened.

Add chicken and pepper. Heat and stir for 2 minutes. Add to pasta.

Add feta cheese and first amount of basil. Stir. Transfer to serving bowl.

*(continued on next page)*

Chicken & Turkey

Garnish with second amount of basil. Makes about 7 1/2 cups (1.9 L).

*1 cup (250 mL): 347 Calories; 11.3 g Total Fat (2.9 g Mono, 0.5 g Poly, 5.6 g Sat);
73 mg Cholesterol; 35 g Carbohydrate; 2 g Fibre; 26 g Protein; 762 mg Sodium*

**Note:** If you do not have any cooked chicken on hand, a roasted chicken from the market is a perfect last-minute time saver.

---

# Bruschetta Chicken

*An appetizer of fussy tomato-topped toasts transforms into a hearty casserole.*

| | | |
|---|---|---|
| Chopped Roma (plum) tomato | 4 cups | 1 L |
| Chopped green onion | 1 1/4 cups | 300 mL |
| Chopped fresh basil | 1/4 cup | 60 mL |
| Garlic cloves, minced | 4 | 4 |
| Olive oil | 1 tbsp. | 15 mL |
| Red wine vinegar | 1 1/2 tsp. | 7 mL |
| Salt | 1/2 tsp. | 2 mL |
| Water | 8 cups | 2 L |
| Salt | 1 tsp. | 5 mL |
| Penne pasta | 2 cups | 500 mL |
| Boneless, skinless chicken thighs (about 3 oz., 85 g, each) | 8 | 8 |
| Box of chicken stove-top stuffing mix | 4 1/4 oz. | 120 g |
| Grated Italian cheese blend | 1 cup | 250 mL |

Combine first 7 ingredients in large bowl. Let stand, covered, for 30 minutes.

Combine water and salt in large saucepan. Bring to a boil. Add pasta. Boil, uncovered, for 10 minutes, stirring occasionally. Drain. Transfer to greased 9 x 13 inch (22 x 33 cm) baking dish.

Arrange chicken thighs over pasta in single layer.

Add stuffing mix to tomato mixture. Stir until moistened. Scatter over chicken. Sprinkle with cheese. Bake, covered, in 375°F (190°C) oven for 30 minutes. Bake, uncovered, for about 30 minutes until browned. Serves 4.

*1 serving: 760 Calories; 28.0 g Total Fat (7.5 g Mono, 3.7 g Poly, 8.2 g Sat); 132 mg
Cholesterol; 75 g Carbohydrate; 6 g Fibre; 50 g Protein; 1101 mg Sodium*

Pictured on page 53.

# Bourbon Chicken Pilaf

*Infuse your pasta with flavour as it boils. Using a pilaf method transforms ordinary pasta into a tangy taste sensation.*

| | | |
|---|---|---|
| Boneless, skinless chicken thighs, cut into bite-sized pieces | 1 lb. | 454 g |
| Sesame oil (for flavour) | 1 tsp. | 5 mL |
| Seasoned salt | 1/4 tsp. | 1 mL |
| Cooking oil | 2 tsp. | 10 mL |
| Chopped onion | 1 cup | 250 mL |
| Garlic cloves, minced (or 1/2 tsp., 2 mL, powder) | 2 | 2 |
| Bourbon whiskey | 1/4 cup | 60 mL |
| Chicken broth | 1 cup | 250 mL |
| Orange juice | 1 cup | 250 mL |
| Maple (or maple-flavoured) syrup | 2 tbsp. | 30 mL |
| Soy sauce | 2 tbsp. | 30 mL |
| Dried crushed chilies | 1/4 tsp. | 1 mL |
| Salt | 1/4 tsp. | 1 mL |
| Pepper | 1/4 tsp. | 1 mL |
| Tiny shell pasta | 1 1/2 cups | 375 mL |
| Chopped red pepper | 2 cups | 500 mL |

Combine first 3 ingredients in small bowl. Heat first amount of cooking oil in large frying pan on medium. Add chicken mixture. Cook for 5 to 8 minutes, stirring occasionally, until browned. Transfer with slotted spoon to separate small bowl. Cover to keep warm.

Add onion and garlic to same frying pan. Cook for 5 to 10 minutes, stirring occasionally, until onion is softened.

Add bourbon. Heat and stir for 30 seconds until liquid is evaporated.

Add next 7 ingredients. Stir. Bring to a boil.

Add pasta and chicken. Stir. Reduce heat to medium-low. Cook, covered, for 15 minutes, stirring often.

Add red pepper. Stir. Cook, covered, for about 5 minutes until pasta is tender but firm. Makes about 6 cups (1.5 L).

*(continued on next page)*

*1 cup (250 mL): 274 Calories; 8.9 g Total Fat (3.1 g Mono, 1.9 g Poly, 1.9 g Sat); 50 mg Cholesterol; 26 g Carbohydrate; 2 g Fibre; 17 g Protein; 798 mg Sodium*

Pictured on page 54.

# Curry Turkey Penne

*If there's a more classic combination than fruit and curry, we've yet to hear it! Banana and apple add sweetness to this hearty dish.*

| | | |
|---|---|---|
| Water | 12 cups | 3 L |
| Salt | 1 1/2 tsp. | 7 mL |
| Penne pasta | 2 1/2 cups | 625 mL |
| Cooking oil | 1 tbsp. | 15 mL |
| Extra-lean ground turkey | 3/4 lb. | 340 g |
| Chopped onion | 1/2 cup | 125 mL |
| Curry powder | 1 tbsp. | 15 mL |
| Garlic cloves, minced | 2 | 2 |
| (or 1/2 tsp., 2 mL, powder) | | |
| Salt | 1/2 tsp. | 2 mL |
| Prepared chicken broth | 1 1/2 cups | 375 mL |
| Diced peeled cooking apple | 1 1/2 cups | 375 mL |
| (such as McIntosh) | | |
| Mashed banana | 1/2 cup | 125 mL |
| Tomato paste (see Tip, page 121) | 2 tbsp. | 30 mL |
| Brown sugar, packed | 1 tsp. | 5 mL |
| Chopped fresh parsley | 1 tbsp. | 15 mL |

Combine water and salt in large saucepan. Bring to a boil. Add pasta. Boil, uncovered, for 14 to 16 minutes, stirring occasionally, until tender but firm. Drain. Return to same pot. Cover to keep warm.

Heat cooking oil in large frying pan on medium. Add next 5 ingredients. Scramble-fry for 5 to 10 minutes until turkey is no longer pink.

Add next 5 ingredients. Stir. Bring to a boil. Reduce heat to medium-low. Simmer for about 15 minutes, stirring occasionally, until apple is soft and mixture has thickened. Add pasta. Toss to coat.

Sprinkle with parsley. Makes about 7 cups (1.75 L).

*1 cup (250 mL): 267 Calories; 3.8 g Total Fat (1.3 g Mono, 0.7 g Poly, 0.3 g Sat); 19 mg Cholesterol; 41 g Carbohydrate; 3 g Fibre; 18 g Protein; 517 mg Sodium*

# Asian Chicken Supreme

*Tomato-sauced pasta spiked with Asian flavours. Fusion cuisine at its finest!*

| | | |
|---|---|---|
| Sesame (or cooking) oil | 1 tbsp. | 15 mL |
| Lean ground chicken | 1 lb. | 454 g |
| Garlic cloves, minced | 3 | 3 |
| (or 3/4 tsp., 4 mL, powder) | | |
| Finely grated gingerroot | 2 tsp. | 10 mL |
| (or 1/2 tsp., 2 mL, ground ginger) | | |
| Pepper | 1/4 tsp. | 1 mL |
| Julienned carrot (see Tip, page 27) | 1 cup | 250 mL |
| Thinly sliced red pepper | 1 cup | 250 mL |
| Thinly sliced onion | 1/2 cup | 125 mL |
| Vegetable broth | 2 cups | 500 mL |
| Spaghettini | 8 oz. | 225 g |
| Can of diced tomato (with juice) | 14 oz. | 398 mL |
| Water | 1 cup | 250 mL |
| Soy sauce | 2 tbsp. | 30 mL |
| Dry-roasted peanuts, chopped | 1/4 cup | 60 mL |
| Chopped green onion | 2 tbsp. | 30 mL |

Heat sesame oil in large frying pan on medium. Add next 4 ingredients. Scramble-fry for 5 to 10 minutes until chicken is no longer pink.

Add next 3 ingredients. Cook for about 3 minutes, stirring occasionally, until onion is starting to soften.

Add next 5 ingredients. Stir. Bring to a boil. Reduce heat to medium-low. Simmer, covered, for about 15 minutes, stirring often, until pasta is tender but firm.

Sprinkle with peanuts and green onion. Makes about 7 1/2 cups (1.9 L).

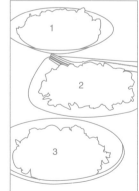

*1 cup (250 mL): 267 Calories; 9.9 g Total Fat (1.2 g Mono, 0.8 g Poly, 2.0 g Sat); 40 mg Cholesterol; 31 g Carbohydrate; 2 g Fibre; 16 g Protein; 721 mg Sodium*

Pictured on page 54.

1. Basa Puttanesca, page 84
2. Lemon Almond Halibut, page 86
3. Cajun Shrimp Tortellini, page 79

Props courtesy of: Wal-Mart Canada Inc.
Danesco Inc.

# Tuna Casserole

*So classic, so comforting! Relive childhood memories with this familiar, family-friendly casserole.*

| | | |
|---|---|---|
| Water | 8 cups | 2 L |
| Salt | 1 tsp. | 5 mL |
| Small shell pasta | 2 1/2 cups | 625 mL |
| Cooking oil | 2 tsp. | 10 mL |
| Chopped onion | 1/2 cup | 125 mL |
| Grated carrot | 1/2 cup | 125 mL |
| Cans of flaked white tuna in water, drained (6 oz., 170 g, each) | 2 | 2 |
| Can of condensed cream of mushroom soup | 10 oz. | 284 mL |
| Milk | 1/2 cup | 125 mL |
| Dijon mustard | 1 tbsp. | 15 mL |
| Dried dillweed | 1 tsp. | 5 mL |
| Grated Cheddar cheese | 1 cup | 250 mL |

Combine water and salt in large saucepan. Bring to a boil. Add pasta. Boil, uncovered, for 8 to 10 minutes, stirring occasionally, until tender but firm. Drain. Transfer to greased 2 quart (2 L) casserole.

Heat cooking oil in medium saucepan on medium. Add onion. Cook, uncovered, for about 3 minutes, stirring often, until starting to soften. Add carrot. Cook, uncovered, for about 2 minutes, stirring often, until softened.

Add next 5 ingredients. Stir. Pour over pasta. Stir until well combined. Bake, covered, in 350°F (175°C) oven for 30 to 40 minutes until bubbling.

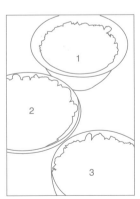

Sprinkle with cheese. Bake, uncovered, for about 5 minutes until cheese is melted. Serves 4.

*1 serving: 469 Calories; 19.6 g Total Fat (4.8 g Mono, 1.9 g Poly, 7.9 g Sat); 71 mg Cholesterol; 38 g Carbohydrate; 1 g Fibre; 34 g Protein; 1083 mg Sodium*

1. Scallop Orzo, page 82
2. Scallop Mushroom Fettuccine, page 81
3. Shrimp Ball Hotpot, page 80

Props courtesy of: Island Pottery Inc.
Pfaltzgraff Canada

# Lemon Cream Salmon

*Salmon gets cozy in a velvety-smooth cream sauce with fresh bursts of lemon.*

| | | |
|---|---|---|
| Water | 12 cups | 3 L |
| Salt | 1 1/2 tsp. | 7 mL |
| Spaghettini | 12 oz. | 340 g |
| Cooking oil | 1 tsp. | 5 mL |
| Finely chopped onion | 1/2 cup | 125 mL |
| Garlic cloves, minced | 2 | 2 |
| (or 1/2 tsp., 2 mL, powder) | | |
| All-purpose flour | 2 tbsp. | 30 mL |
| Prepared chicken broth | 1 cup | 250 mL |
| Half-and-half cream | 1 1/2 cups | 375 mL |
| Salt | 1/2 tsp. | 2 mL |
| Pepper | 1/4 tsp. | 1 mL |
| Salmon fillets, skin removed, cut into | 1 lb. | 454 g |
| 1/4 inch (6 mm) thick strips | | |
| Chopped fresh parsley | 1 tbsp. | 30 mL |
| Grated lemon zest | 1 tbsp. | 30 mL |

Combine water and salt in Dutch oven. Bring to a boil. Add pasta. Boil, uncovered, for 9 to 11 minutes, stirring occasionally, until tender but firm. Drain. Return to same pot. Cover to keep warm.

Heat cooking oil in large frying pan on medium. Add onion and garlic. Cook for about 5 minutes, stirring often, until onion is softened.

Add flour. Heat and stir for 1 minute. Slowly add broth, stirring constantly, until boiling and thickened. Add next 3 ingredients. Stir.

Add salmon. Simmer for 3 to 5 minutes, stirring occasionally, until salmon flakes easily when tested with a fork. Add to pasta.

Sprinkle with parsley and lemon zest. Toss gently to combine. Makes about 7 cups (1.75 L).

*1 cup (250 mL): 378 Calories; 14.3 g Total Fat (5.0 g Mono, 2.3 g Poly, 5.8 g Sat);*
*51 mg Cholesterol; 42 g Carbohydrate; trace Fibre; 21 g Protein; 432 mg Sodium*

Fish & Seafood

# Herbed Clam Linguine

*There's a reason some things become classics—take the combination of white wine, clams and mushrooms, for example. An elegant pairing of flavours, yet this dish is so simple to make. You'll want to have it again and again.*

| | | |
|---|---|---|
| Water | 12 cups | 3 L |
| Salt | 1 1/2 tsp. | 7 mL |
| Linguine | 12 oz. | 340 g |
| Olive (or cooking) oil | 1 tbsp. | 15 mL |
| Chopped green onion | 2/3 cup | 150 mL |
| Garlic cloves, minced (or 3/4 tsp., 4 mL, powder) | 3 | 3 |
| Dry (or alcohol-free) white wine | 1 cup | 250 mL |
| Prepared chicken broth | 1 cup | 250 mL |
| Reserved clam liquid | 1 cup | 250 mL |
| Sliced fresh white mushrooms | 1 cup | 250 mL |
| Dried basil | 1 tsp. | 5 mL |
| Dried oregano | 1 tsp. | 5 mL |
| Dried thyme | 1/2 tsp. | 2 mL |
| Cans of whole baby clams (5 oz., 142 g, each), drained and liquid reserved | 2 | 2 |
| Block of cream cheese, cut-up, softened | 8 oz. | 250 g |
| Grated Romano cheese | 1/4 cup | 60 mL |

Combine water and salt in Dutch oven. Bring to a boil. Add pasta. Boil, uncovered, for 9 to 11 minutes, stirring occasionally, until tender but firm. Drain. Return to same pot. Cover to keep warm.

Heat olive oil in large saucepan on medium. Add green onion and garlic. Cook, uncovered, for about 2 minutes, stirring often, until onion is softened.

Add next 7 ingredients. Stir. Bring to a boil. Reduce heat to medium-low. Simmer, uncovered, for 20 minutes.

Add clams and cream cheese. Heat and stir for 5 to 7 minutes until cream cheese is melted.

Add Romano cheese and pasta. Toss. Let stand for 5 minutes. Makes about 8 1/2 cups (2.1 L).

*1 cup (250 mL): 337 Calories; 14.0 g Total Fat (1.2 g Mono, 0.3 g Poly, 6.9 g Sat); 58 mg Cholesterol; 34 g Carbohydrate; 2 g Fibre; 14 g Protein; 430 mg Sodium*

# Shrimp Jambalaya Penne

*When it comes to jambalaya, rice is nice but pasta is perfect! Serve this spicy sausage delight with a bottle of hot sauce on the side for those who dare.*

| | | |
|---|---|---|
| Cooking oil | 2 tsp. | 10 mL |
| Chorizo sausage, casing removed | 1/2 lb. | 225 g |
| Chopped celery | 1 cup | 250 mL |
| Chopped green pepper | 1 cup | 250 mL |
| Chopped onion | 1 cup | 250 mL |
| Garlic cloves, minced | 2 | 2 |
| (or 1/2 tsp., 2 mL, powder) | | |
| Dried basil | 1 tsp. | 5 mL |
| Dried oregano | 1 tsp. | 5 mL |
| Ground cumin | 1 tsp. | 5 mL |
| Cayenne pepper | 1/4 tsp. | 1 mL |
| Ground allspice | 1/4 tsp. | 1 mL |
| Can of diced tomatoes (with juice) | 28 oz. | 796 mL |
| Can of tomato sauce | 7 1/2 oz. | 213 mL |
| Bay leaves | 2 | 2 |
| Water | 12 cups | 3 L |
| Salt | 1 1/2 tsp. | 7 mL |
| Penne pasta | 3 1/2 cups | 875 mL |
| Uncooked medium shrimp | 1 lb. | 454 g |
| (peeled and deveined) | | |

Heat cooking oil in large frying pan on medium. Add sausage. Scramble-fry for about 5 minutes until starting to brown.

Add next 9 ingredients. Stir. Cook for 5 to 10 minutes, stirring occasionally, until vegetables are almost tender.

Add next 3 ingredients. Bring to a boil. Simmer, uncovered, for about 10 minutes until sauce has thickened.

Combine water and salt in Dutch oven. Bring to a boil. Add pasta. Boil, uncovered, for 13 minutes, stirring occasionally.

Add shrimp. Cook, uncovered, for about 2 minutes until shrimp turn pink and pasta is tender but firm. Drain. Add sausage mixture. Toss. Makes about 10 cups (2.5 L).

*1 cup (250 mL): 344 Calories; 11.2 g Total Fat (4.8 g Mono, 1.4 g Poly, 3.5 g Sat); 89 mg Cholesterol; 39 g Carbohydrate; 2 g Fibre; 21 g Protein; 693 mg Sodium*

# Salmon Cannelloni

*Tender tubes of fresh pasta are stuffed with creamy dill, salmon and spinach.*
*Store-bought ingredients make for a meal that's as easy as it is elegant!*

| | | |
|---|---|---|
| Salmon fillets, skin removed, cut into 1/4 inch (6 mm) pieces | 1 lb. | 454 g |
| Chopped fresh spinach leaves | 2 cups | 500 mL |
| Smoked salmon cream cheese | 1/2 cup | 125 mL |
| Chopped fresh dill (or 3/4 tsp., 4 mL, dried) | 1 tbsp. | 15 mL |
| Lemon juice | 1 tbsp. | 15 mL |
| Salt | 1/2 tsp | 2 mL |
| Pepper | 1/4 tsp. | 1 mL |
| Rosé pasta sauce | 1 cup | 250 mL |
| Fresh lasagna sheets (about 6 x 8 inches, 15 x 20 cm, each), see Note | 4 | 4 |
| Rosé pasta sauce | 1 1/2 cups | 375 mL |

Combine first 7 ingredients in large bowl. Stir.

Spread first amount of pasta sauce in greased 8 x 8 inch (20 x 20 cm) baking dish.

Cut lasagna sheets in half crosswise into 6 x 4 inch (15 x 10 cm) rectangles. Soak in warm water for about 2 minutes until softened. Pat dry.

Spread about 1/3 cup (75 mL) salmon mixture over 1 pasta rectangle, leaving 1 inch (2.5 cm) space along 1 short edge. Roll up, jelly roll-style, from opposite short edge. Place, seam-side down, in baking dish. Repeat with remaining pasta and salmon mixture. Pour second amount of pasta sauce over rolls. Bake, covered, in 350°F (175°C) oven for about 50 minutes until salmon is cooked and pasta is tender. Let stand, uncovered, for 10 minutes. Makes 8 cannelloni.

*1 cannelloni: 272 Calories; 15.6 g Total Fat (2.5 g Mono, 1.6 g Poly, 7.1 g Sat); 58 mg Cholesterol; 16 g Carbohydrate; 2 g Fibre; 15 g Protein; 516 mg Sodium*

**Note:** You may use fresh homemade pasta instead of purchased pasta sheets.

# Fusilli Cioppino

*The classic cioppino (pronounced chuh-PEE-noh) is a soup, but as we've seen, lots of classic dishes easily lend their flavours to pasta. The combination of red wine, tomato and seafood makes a splendid sauce.*

| | | |
|---|---|---|
| Olive (or cooking) oil | 2 tsp. | 10 mL |
| Chopped onion | 1 cup | 250 mL |
| Garlic cloves, minced | 3 | 3 |
| (or 3/4 tsp., 4 mL, powder) | | |
| Dried basil | 1/2 tsp. | 2 mL |
| Dried oregano | 1/2 tsp. | 2 mL |
| Dried crushed chilies | 1/4 tsp. | 1 mL |
| Dry (or alcohol-free) white wine | 1 cup | 250 mL |
| Can of diced tomatoes (with juice) | 28 oz. | 796 mL |
| Prepared chicken broth | 1 1/2 cups | 375 mL |
| Reserved liquid from clams | 2/3 cup | 150 mL |
| Tomato paste (see Tip, page 121) | 1 tbsp. | 15 mL |
| Granulated sugar | 1/2 tsp. | 2 mL |
| Salt | 1/2 tsp. | 2 mL |
| Pepper | 1/4 tsp. | 1 mL |
| Fusilli pasta | 2 cups | 500 mL |
| Can of whole baby clams, drained | 5 oz. | 142 g |
| and liquid reserved | | |
| Uncooked small shrimp | 1/2 lb. | 225 g |
| (peeled and deveined) | | |

Heat olive oil in Dutch oven on medium. Add next 5 ingredients. Cook, uncovered, for 5 to 10 minutes, stirring often, until onion is softened.

Add wine. Simmer, uncovered, for 2 minutes.

Add next 7 ingredients. Stir. Bring to a boil.

Add pasta. Stir. Reduce heat to medium-low. Cook, covered, for about 10 minutes, stirring often, until tender but firm. Increase heat to medium. Add clams and shrimp. Heat and stir for about 2 minutes until shrimp turn pink. Makes about 8 cups (2 L).

*1 cup (250 mL): 176 Calories; 2.7 g Total Fat (0.9 g Mono, 0.4 g Poly, 0.4 g Sat); 57 mg Cholesterol; 21 g Carbohydrate; 1 g Fibre; 12 g Protein; 728 mg Sodium*

Fish & Seafood

# Cajun Shrimp Tortellini

*Bring some life back to your dinner table with this vibrant blend of tortellini, shrimp and fresh tomatoes. For variation, try using short pasta such as fusilli.*

| | | |
|---|---|---|
| Water | 12 cups | 3 L |
| Salt | 1 1/2 tsp. | 7 mL |
| Package of fresh cheese tortellini | 12 1/2 oz. | 340 g |
| Medium uncooked shrimp (peeled and deveined) | 3/4 lb. | 340 g |
| Cooking oil | 2 tsp. | 10 mL |
| Cajun seasoning | 1 tsp. | 5 mL |
| Bacon slices, chopped | 4 | 4 |
| Chopped onion | 1/2 cup | 125 mL |
| Garlic cloves, minced (or 1/2 tsp., 2 mL, powder) | 2 | 2 |
| Chopped sun-dried tomatoes in oil, blotted dry | 1/4 cup | 60 mL |
| Salt | 1/4 tsp. | 1 mL |
| Pepper | 1/8 tsp. | 0.5 mL |
| Chopped Roma (plum) tomato | 2 cups | 500 mL |
| Olive oil | 1 tbsp. | 15 mL |

Combine water and salt in Dutch oven. Bring to a boil. Add pasta. Boil, uncovered, for 8 to 11 minutes, stirring occasionally, until tender. Drain. Return to same pot. Cover to keep warm.

Combine next 3 ingredients in small bowl. Set aside.

Combine next 3 ingredients in large frying pan on medium. Cook for 5 to 8 minutes, stirring often, until onion is softened.

Add next 3 ingredients and shrimp mixture. Cook for about 2 minutes, stirring occasionally, until shrimp turn pink. Add to pasta. Toss.

Add tomato and olive oil. Toss. Makes about 8 cups (2 L).

*1 cup (250 mL): 273 Calories; 12.0 g Total Fat (5.2 g Mono, 1.7 g Poly, 3.7 g Sat); 90 mg Cholesterol; 25 g Carbohydrate; 2 g Fibre; 17 g Protein; 482 mg Sodium*

Pictured on page 71.

# Shrimp Ball Hotpot

*Think small! Tiny bow pasta and shrimp balls in a soy and ginger-flavoured broth that's really big on taste.*

| | | |
|---|---|---|
| Uncooked shrimp (peeled and deveined) | 3/4 lb. | 340 g |
| Canned sliced water chestnuts | 1/4 cup | 60 mL |
| Chopped fresh cilantro | 2 tsp. | 10 mL |
| Cornstarch | 2 tsp. | 10 mL |
| Rice vinegar | 1 tsp. | 5 mL |
| Soy sauce | 1 tsp. | 5 mL |
| Ground ginger | 1/2 tsp. | 2 mL |
| Garlic powder | 1/4 tsp. | 1 mL |
| Salt | 1/2 tsp. | 2 mL |
| Pepper | 1/4 tsp. | 1 mL |
| Prepared vegetable broth | 2 1/2 cups | 625 mL |
| Gingerroot slices, about 1/4 inch (6 mm) thick | 2 | 2 |
| Star anise | 1 | 1 |
| Tiny bow pasta | 1 1/2 cups | 375 mL |
| Snow peas, trimmed and halved | 2 cups | 500 mL |
| Chopped red pepper | 1 cup | 250 mL |

Put first 10 ingredients into food processor. Process with on/off motion until shrimp is coarsely chopped. Shape into 3/4 inch (2 cm) balls. Set aside.

Combine next 3 ingredients in large saucepan. Bring to a boil. Add pasta. Stir. Boil gently, covered, on medium for 6 to 8 minutes, stirring often, until almost tender.

Add snow peas, red pepper and shrimp balls. Stir gently. Cook, covered, for 5 to 10 minutes, stirring often, until pasta is tender but firm. Remove and discard gingerroot and star anise. Makes about 6 cups (1.5 L).

*1 cup (250 mL): 213 Calories; 1.7 g Total Fat (0.2 g Mono, 0.5 g Poly, 0.2 g Sat); 86 mg Cholesterol; 31 g Carbohydrate; 3 g Fibre; 17 g Protein; 747 mg Sodium*

Pictured on page 72.

# Scallop Mushroom Fettuccine

*The flavours of white wine, Parmesan and scallops add panache to this simple, satisfying dish.*

| | | |
|---|---|---|
| Water | 12 cups | 3 L |
| Salt | 1 1/2 tsp. | 7 mL |
| Fettuccine | 8 oz. | 225 g |
| Olive (or cooking) oil | 1 tbsp. | 15 mL |
| Sliced fresh white mushrooms | 4 cups | 1 L |
| Garlic clove, minced (or 1/4 tsp., 1 mL, powder) | 1 | 1 |
| Dry (or alcohol-free) white wine | 1/4 cup | 60 mL |
| Butter (or hard margarine) | 2 tbsp. | 30 mL |
| Lemon juice | 1 tbsp. | 15 mL |
| Small bay scallops | 1 lb. | 454 g |
| Grated Parmesan cheese | 1/2 cup | 125 mL |
| Sliced green onion | 3 tbsp. | 50 mL |
| Grated lemon zest (see Tip, below) | 1 tbsp. | 15 mL |
| Salt | 1/4 tsp. | 1 mL |

Combine water and salt in Dutch oven. Bring to a boil. Add pasta. Boil, uncovered, for 11 to 13 minutes, stirring occasionally, until tender but firm. Drain. Return to same pot. Cover to keep warm.

Heat olive oil in large frying pan on medium. Add mushrooms and garlic. Cook for about 5 minutes, stirring occasionally, until liquid has evaporated.

Add next 3 ingredients. Heat and stir until butter melts. Add scallops. Heat and stir for about 2 minutes until scallops are opaque.

Add remaining 4 ingredients and pasta. Toss. Makes about 6 cups (1.5 L).

*1 cup (250 mL): 323 Calories; 10.4 g Total Fat (2.7 g Mono, 0.7 g Poly, 4.8 g Sat); 45 mg Cholesterol; 33 g Carbohydrate; 2 g Fibre; 23 g Protein; 419 mg Sodium*

Pictured on page 72.

 *tip* When a recipe calls for grated citrus zest and juice, it's easier to grate the fruit first, then juice it. Be careful not to grate down to the pith (white part of the peel), which is bitter and best avoided.

# Scallop Orzo

*Tender scallops are embedded in fluffy orzo pasta with the fresh flavours of asparagus, shiitake mushrooms and a hint of fennel.*

| | | |
|---|---|---|
| Water | 8 cups | 2 L |
| Salt | 1 tsp. | 5 mL |
| Orzo | 1 1/2 cups | 375 mL |
| Cooking oil | 2 tsp. | 10 mL |
| Chopped onion | 1 cup | 250 mL |
| Garlic cloves, minced | 2 | 2 |
| (or 1/2 tsp., 2 mL, powder) | | |
| Finely grated gingerroot | 1 tsp. | 5 mL |
| Dried crushed chilies | 1/4 tsp. | 1 mL |
| Fennel seed | 1/4 tsp. | 1 mL |
| Diced red pepper | 1 1/2 cups | 375 mL |
| Small bay scallops | 3/4 lb. | 340 g |
| Chopped fresh asparagus | 1 cup | 250 mL |
| Chopped fresh shiitake mushrooms | 1 cup | 250 mL |
| Salt | 1/2 tsp. | 2 mL |
| Pepper | 1/4 tsp. | 1 mL |

Combine water and salt in large saucepan. Bring to a boil. Add pasta. Boil, uncovered, for 8 to 10 minutes, stirring occasionally, until tender but firm. Drain. Return to same pot. Cover to keep warm.

Heat cooking oil in large frying pan on medium. Add next 5 ingredients. Cook for 5 to 10 minutes, stirring often, until onion is softened.

Add remaining 6 ingredients. Cook and stir for 4 minutes. Add pasta. Heat and stir for about 2 minutes until scallops turn opaque. Makes about 6 cups (1.5 L).

*1 cup (250 mL): 260 Calories; 2.7 g Total Fat (1.0 g Mono, 0.7 g Poly, 0.2 g Sat); 19 mg Cholesterol; 42 g Carbohydrate; 4 g Fibre; 16 g Protein; 288 mg Sodium*

Pictured on page 72.

# Coconut Curry Shrimp

*Coconut, curry and shrimp—oh, my! Sweet, creamy and savoury ingredients come together to create something wonderful.*

| | | |
|---|---|---|
| Water | 8 cups | 2 L |
| Salt | 1 tsp. | 5 mL |
| Rotini pasta | 3 cups | 750 mL |
| Bag of frozen uncooked large shrimp (peeled and deveined), thawed | 12 oz. | 340 g |
| Cooking oil | 1 tsp. | 5 mL |
| Chopped onion | 1 cup | 250 mL |
| Garlic clove, minced (or 1/4 tsp., 1 mL, powder) | 1 | 1 |
| Curry powder | 1 tsp. | 5 mL |
| Diced, peeled orange-fleshed sweet potato | 1 cup | 250 mL |
| Thinly sliced green pepper | 1 cup | 250 mL |
| Can of light coconut milk | 14 oz. | 398 mL |
| Prepared vegetable broth | 1/2 cup | 125 mL |
| Salt | 1/2 tsp. | 2 mL |

Combine water and salt in large saucepan. Bring to a boil. Add pasta. Boil, uncovered, for 9 minutes, stirring occasionally. Add shrimp. Cook for 2 to 4 minutes, stirring occasionally, until pasta is tender but firm and shrimp turn pink. Drain. Return to same pot. Cover to keep warm.

Heat cooking oil in large frying pan on medium. Add next 3 ingredients. Cook for about 5 minutes, stirring occasionally, until onion starts to soften.

Add sweet potato and green pepper. Cook for about 5 minutes, stirring occasionally, until sweet potato is almost tender.

Add remaining three ingredients. Bring to a boil. Simmer for 5 minutes to blend flavours. Add to pasta mixture. Stir. Makes about 7 cups (1.75 L).

*1 cup (250 mL): 249 Calories; 8.2 g Total Fat (0.8 g Mono, 0.6 g Poly, 5.6 g Sat); 74 mg Cholesterol; 29 g Carbohydrate; 3 g Fibre; 15 g Protein; 286 mg Sodium*

# Basa Puttanesca

*Don't think you're an anchovy person? This Puttanesca
(pronounced poot-tah-NEHS-kah) has subtle anchovy flavour with big
chunks of tender basa for an updated version of this Italian favourite.*

| | | |
|---|---|---|
| Water | 8 cups | 2 L |
| Salt | 1 tsp. | 5 mL |
| Cavatappi pasta | 3 cups | 750 mL |
| Olive oil | 1 tbsp. | 15 mL |
| Chopped onion | 1 cup | 250 mL |
| Garlic cloves, minced | 3 | 3 |
| (or 3/4 tsp., 4 mL, powder) | | |
| Can of tomato pasta sauce | 23 oz. | 680 mL |
| Can of diced tomatoes (with juice) | 14 oz. | 398 mL |
| Sliced kalamata olives | 1/2 cup | 125 mL |
| Capers | 2 tbsp. | 30 mL |
| Chopped fresh basil | 2 tbsp. | 30 mL |
| (or 1 1/2 tsp., 7 mL, dried) | | |
| Granulated sugar | 1 tbsp. | 15 mL |
| Anchovy paste | 1 tsp. | 5 mL |
| Dried crushed chilies | 1/2 tsp. | 2 mL |
| Cayenne pepper | 1/8 tsp. | 0.5 mL |
| Basa fillets, any small bones removed, | 3/4 lb. | 340 g |
| cut into 1 1/2 inch (3.8 cm) pieces | | |
| Grated Romano cheese | 2 tbsp. | 30 mL |
| Chopped fresh basil | 1 tbsp. | 15 mL |

Combine water and salt in large saucepan. Bring to a boil. Add pasta. Boil,
uncovered, for 10 to 12 minutes, stirring occasionally, until tender but firm.
Drain. Return to same pot. Cover to keep warm.

Heat olive oil in large frying pan on medium. Add onion. Cook for 5 to
10 minutes, stirring often, until starting to turn golden. Add garlic. Heat
and stir for 1 minute.

Add next 9 ingredients. Stir. Bring to a boil. Reduce heat to medium-low.
Simmer, uncovered, for about 10 minutes, stirring occasionally, until
flavours are blended.

*(continued on next page)*

Fish & Seafood

Add fish. Stir. Cook for about 5 minutes until fish flakes easily when tested with fork. Add to pasta. Stir gently. Transfer to serving bowl.

Sprinkle with cheese and second amount of basil. Makes about 8 cups (2 L).

*1 cup (250 mL): 226 Calories; 6.0 g Total Fat (1.9 g Mono, 0.4 g Poly, 1.5 g Sat); 21 mg Cholesterol; 33 g Carbohydrate; 3 g Fibre; 12 g Protein; 846 mg Sodium*

Pictured on page 71.

# Lemon Pesto Shrimp

*With pink shrimp and a pale green pesto sauce flecked with bits of yellow lemon zest, this might just be the prettiest pasta you've ever eaten!*

| | | |
|---|---|---|
| Water | 12 cups | 3 L |
| Salt | 1 1/2 tsp. | 7 mL |
| Angel hair pasta | 8 oz. | 225 g |
| Bag of frozen uncooked medium shrimp (peeled and deveined), thawed | 12 oz. | 340 g |
| Basil pesto (or Classic Pesto Sauce, page 134) | 1/2 cup | 125 mL |
| Half-and-half cream | 1/4 cup | 60 mL |
| Lemon juice | 1 tbsp. | 15 mL |
| Grated lemon zest (see Tip, page 81) | 2 tsp. | 10 mL |
| Grated Parmesan cheese | 1/4 cup | 60 mL |

Combine water and salt in Dutch oven. Bring to a boil. Add pasta. Boil, uncovered, for 3 minutes, stirring occasionally. Add shrimp. Cook, uncovered, for about 2 minutes, stirring occasionally, until pasta is tender but firm and shrimp are pink. Drain, reserving 1/2 cup (125 mL) cooking water. Return pasta and shrimp to same pot. Cover to keep warm.

Combine remaining 4 ingredients and reserved cooking water in small bowl. Add to pasta.

Add cheese. Toss. Makes about 5 cups (1.25 L).

*1 cup (250 mL): 408 Calories; 17.6 g Total Fat (0.6 g Mono, 0.5 g Poly, 4.3 g Sat); 120 mg Cholesterol; 35 g Carbohydrate; 1 g Fibre; 25 g Protein; 420 mg Sodium*

# Lemon Almond Halibut

*Feel like something not too heavy? Lighten up with the delicate flavours of lemon and halibut with crunchy almonds and salty capers.*

| | | |
|---|---|---|
| Water | 8 cups | 2 L |
| Salt | 1 tsp. | 5 mL |
| Small shell pasta | 2 cups | 500 mL |
| All-purpose flour | 3 tbsp. | 50 mL |
| Lemon pepper | 1 1/2 tsp. | 7 mL |
| Salt | 1/4 tsp. | 1 mL |
| Halibut fillets, any small bones removed, cut into 1 inch (2.5 cm) pieces | 1 lb. | 454 g |
| Cooking oil | 1 tbsp. | 15 mL |
| Butter (or hard margarine) | 1 tbsp. | 15 mL |
| Dry (or alcohol-free) white wine | 1/4 cup | 60 mL |
| Vegetable broth | 3/4 cup | 175 mL |
| Lemon juice | 3 tbsp. | 50 mL |
| Chopped green onion | 1/3 cup | 75 mL |
| Grated lemon zest (see Tip, page 81) | 1 tbsp. | 15 mL |
| Slivered almonds, toasted (see Tip, page 104) | 1/2 cup | 125 mL |
| Capers (optional) | 2 tbsp. | 30 mL |

Combine water and salt in large saucepan. Bring to a boil. Add pasta. Boil, uncovered, for 8 to 10 minutes, stirring occasionally, until tender but firm. Drain. Return to same pot. Cover to keep warm.

Combine next 3 ingredients in large resealable freezer bag. Add fish. Toss until coated.

Heat cooking oil and butter in large frying pan on medium. Add fish. Discard any remaining flour mixture. Cook for about 5 minutes, turning occasionally, until browned and fish flakes easily when tested with a fork. Add to pasta with slotted spoon. Cover to keep warm.

Add wine to same frying pan. Cook and stir, scraping any brown bits from bottom of pan, for 1 minute. Add next 4 ingredients. Bring to a boil. Add pasta mixture. Toss gently.

Sprinkle with almonds and capers. Makes about 6 cups (1.5 L).

*1 cup (250 mL): 275 Calories; 11.1 g Total Fat (5.3 g Mono, 2.4 g Poly, 2.0 g Sat); 29 mg Cholesterol; 22 g Carbohydrate; 1 g Fibre; 21 g Protein; 225 mg Sodium*

Pictured on page 71.

# Tex-Mex Penne

*There's something fishy going on here—and that's a good thing! Even people who don't like fish will be persuaded to give it another try when it's paired with pasta and covered in salsa and cheese.*

| | | |
|---|---|---|
| Water | 8 cups | 2 L |
| Salt | 1 tsp. | 5 mL |
| Penne pasta | 2 cups | 500 mL |
| Medium chunky salsa | 1 cup | 250 mL |
| Haddock fillets, any small bones removed, cut into bite-sized pieces | 1 lb. | 454 g |
| Salt | 1/2 tsp. | 2 mL |
| Pepper | 1/4 tsp. | 1 mL |
| Medium chunky salsa | 1 cup | 250 mL |
| Grated jalapeño Monterey Jack cheese | 1 1/2 cups | 375 mL |

Combine water and salt in large saucepan. Bring to a boil. Add pasta. Boil, uncovered, for 14 to 16 minutes, stirring occasionally, until tender but firm. Drain. Return to same pot.

Add first amount of salsa. Toss. Spread in even layer in bottom of greased 2 quart (2 L) baking dish.

Arrange fish in single layer over pasta mixture. Sprinkle with salt and pepper.

Spread second amount of salsa over fish. Sprinkle with cheese. Bake, uncovered, in 375°F (190°C) oven for about 40 minutes until fish flakes easily with fork and cheese is golden. Serves 4.

*1 serving: 503 Calories; 15.3 g Total Fat (0.1 g Mono, 0.3 g Poly, 7.7 g Sat); 102 mg Cholesterol; 56 g Carbohydrate; 2 g Fibre; 38 g Protein; 1573 mg Sodium*

## Paré Pointer

*When they told him the meal was on the house, he went up on the roof to eat.*

# Bows, Broccoli And Scallops

*Tender, sweet scallops are done up right in this blend of bow-tie pasta and broccoli in an herb and garlic cream sauce.*

| | | |
|---|---|---|
| Water | 8 cups | 2 L |
| Salt | 1 tsp. | 5 mL |
| Medium bow pasta | 3 cups | 750 mL |
| Broccoli florets | 3 cups | 750 mL |
| Butter (or hard margarine) | 1 tbsp. | 15 mL |
| All-purpose flour | 4 tsp. | 20 mL |
| Prepared chicken (or vegetable) broth | 1 1/2 cups | 375 mL |
| Herb and garlic spreadable cream cheese | 1/2 cup | 125 mL |
| Large sea scallops, cut in half crosswise | 1 lb. | 454 g |

Combine water and salt in large saucepan. Bring to a boil. Add pasta. Boil, uncovered, for 8 minutes, stirring occasionally. Add broccoli. Cook, uncovered, for 2 to 4 minutes, stirring occasionally, until pasta is tender but firm and broccoli is tender-crisp. Drain. Return to same pot. Cover to keep warm.

Heat butter in separate large saucepan on medium. Add flour. Heat and stir for 1 minute. Gradually add broth, whisking constantly until smooth. Heat and stir until boiling and thickened. Add cream cheese. Whisk until smooth. Add scallops. Stir. Simmer, uncovered, for 2 to 4 minutes until scallops are opaque. Add pasta mixture. Stir until coated. Makes about 7 cups (1.75 L).

*1 cup (250 mL): 266 Calories; 7.1 g Total Fat (0.5 g Mono, 0.4 g Poly, 3.7 g Sat); 43 mg Cholesterol; 32 g Carbohydrate; 2 g Fibre; 18 g Protein; 519 mg Sodium*

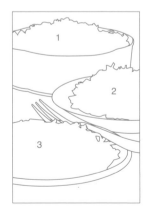

1.  Fresh Tomato Spinach Pasta, page 97
2.  Springtime Pasta, page 103
3.  Pepper And Kale Linguine, page 98

Props courtesy of:  Cherison Enterprises Inc.
Casa Bugatti

# Cheesy Pasta Bake

*Think turkey casserole—without the turkey! This satisfyingly cheesy dish will be a favourite with kids and adults alike.*

| | | |
|---|---|---|
| Water | 12 cups | 3 L |
| Salt | 1 1/2 tsp. | 7 mL |
| Small shell pasta | 2 cups | 500 mL |
| Chopped onion | 1 cup | 250 mL |
| Can of condensed cream of mushroom soup | 10 oz. | 284 mL |
| Mayonnaise | 1/2 cup | 125 mL |
| Milk | 1/4 cup | 60 mL |
| Grated medium Cheddar cheese | 3 cups | 750 mL |
| Worcestershire sauce | 2 tsp. | 10 mL |
| Jar of sliced pimiento, well drained (optional) | 2 oz. | 57 mL |

Combine water and salt in Dutch oven. Bring to a boil. Add pasta and onion. Boil, uncovered, for 8 to 10 minutes, stirring occasionally, until pasta is tender but firm. Drain. Return to same pot.

Combine next 3 ingredients in medium bowl. Add to pasta mixture. Stir.

Add remaining 3 ingredients. Stir well. Transfer to greased 2 quart (2 L) casserole. Bake, uncovered, in 350°F (175°C) oven for about 30 minutes until heated through and golden. Makes about 7 cups (1.75 L).

*1 cup (250 mL): 421 Calories; 31.5 g Total Fat (4.6 g Mono, 0.5 g Poly, 12.5 g Sat); 59 mg Cholesterol; 19 g Carbohydrate; 1 g Fibre; 15 g Protein; 699 mg Sodium*

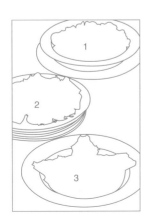

1. Nutty Edamame Shells, page 100
2. Creamy Tomato Shiitake Rigatoni, page 95
3. Bean-Stuffed Shells, page 101

Props courtesy of: Pfaltzgraff Canada

Meatless

# Roasted Vegetable Pasta

*Mellow roasted vegetables, garlic and rosemary give such depth of flavour to this simple pasta dish! For variation, roast the veggies in a grill pan on the barbecue.*

| | | |
|---|---|---|
| Cubed asian eggplant (with peel),<br>1 1/2 inch (3.8 cm) pieces | 4 cups | 1 L |
| Cubed zucchini (with peel),<br>1 1/2 inch (3.8 cm) pieces | 4 cups | 1 L |
| Chopped red pepper<br>(1 inch, 2.5 cm, pieces) | 2 1/2 cups | 625 mL |
| Chopped red onion<br>(1 inch, 2.5 cm, pieces) | 1 cup | 250 mL |
| Cherry tomatoes | 24 | 24 |
| Olive oil | 1/4 cup | 60 mL |
| Finely chopped fresh rosemary<br>(or 3/4 tsp, 4 mL, dried, crushed) | 1 tbsp. | 15 mL |
| Garlic cloves, minced<br>(or 1/2 tsp., 2 mL, powder) | 2 | 2 |
| Coarsely ground pepper | 1/2 tsp. | 2 mL |
| Water | 8 cups | 2 L |
| Salt | 1 tsp. | 5 mL |
| Rigatoni pasta | 2 1/2 cups | 625 mL |
| Grated Romano cheese | 1/2 cup | 125 mL |
| Salt | 3/4 tsp. | 4 mL |

Combine first 5 ingredients in large bowl.

Combine next 4 ingredients in small cup. Drizzle over vegetables. Toss to coat. Spread evenly on ungreased baking sheet with sides. Bake in 425°F (220°C) oven for about 20 minutes, stirring at halftime, until vegetables are softened and starting to brown.

Combine water and salt in large saucepan. Bring to a boil. Add pasta. Boil, uncovered, for 14 to 16 minutes, stirring occasionally, until tender but firm. Drain, reserving 1/2 cup (125 mL) cooking water. Return pasta and cooking water to same pot.

Add roasted vegetables, cheese and salt. Toss. Makes about 9 cups (2.25 L).

*1 cup (250 mL): 193 Calories; 9.0 g Total Fat (4.5 g Mono, 1.1 g Poly, 2.3 g Sat); 7 mg Cholesterol; 24 g Carbohydrate; 4 g Fibre; 7 g Protein; 317 mg Sodium*

Meatless

# Fusilli Vegetable Frittata

*This flavourful frittata is a great way to use up leftover cooked pasta and those odd bits of vegetables lurking in the back of the refrigerator.*

| | | |
|---|---|---|
| Cooking oil | 1 tbsp. | 15 mL |
| Sliced fresh white mushrooms | 1 cup | 250 mL |
| Chopped onion | 1/3 cup | 75 mL |
| Broccoli florets, chopped | 1 cup | 250 mL |
| Diced zucchini (with peel) | 2/3 cup | 150 mL |
| Diced red pepper | 1/3 cup | 75 mL |
| Cooked fusilli pasta (about 1 1/2 cups, 375 mL, uncooked) | 2 cups | 500 mL |
| Large eggs, fork-beaten | 6 | 6 |
| Milk | 1/2 cup | 125 mL |
| Sun-dried tomato pesto | 1 tbsp. | 15 mL |
| Salt | 1/2 tsp. | 2 mL |
| Pepper | 1/8 tsp. | 0.5 mL |
| Grated Italian cheese blend | 1 1/2 cups | 375 mL |

Heat cooking oil in large frying pan on medium. Add mushrooms and onion. Cook for 5 to 10 minutes, stirring occasionally, until onion is softened and mushrooms are starting to brown.

Add next 3 ingredients. Stir. Cook for about 5 minutes until vegetables are tender-crisp. Add pasta. Stir.

Whisk next 5 ingredients in medium bowl. Add to pasta mixture. Stir. Reduce heat to medium-low. Cook, covered, for about 5 minutes until bottom is golden and top is almost set. Remove from heat.

Sprinkle with cheese. Broil on top rack in oven for about 3 minutes until frittata is golden and set (see Note). Serves 4.

*1 serving: 404 Calories; 21.7 g Total Fat (2.1 g Mono, 1.1 g Poly, 8.7 g Sat); 354 mg Cholesterol; 29 g Carbohydrate; 2 g Fibre; 25 g Protein; 871 mg Sodium*

**Note:** When baking or broiling food in a frying pan with a handle that isn't ovenproof, wrap the handle in foil and keep it to the front of the oven, away from the element.

# Ricotta Roll-Ups

*Let the good times roll with these pasta spirals stuffed with a creamy cheese filling.*

| | | |
|---|---|---|
| Water | 12 cups | 3 L |
| Salt | 1 1/2 tsp. | 7 mL |
| Spinach lasagna noodles | 8 | 8 |
| Cooking oil | 2 tsp. | 10 mL |
| Chopped fresh white mushrooms | 2 cups | 500 mL |
| Finely chopped onion | 1 cup | 250 mL |
| Ricotta cheese | 1 1/2 cups | 375 mL |
| Grated mozzarella cheese | 1 cup | 250 mL |
| Grated Parmesan cheese | 1/2 cup | 125 mL |
| Salt | 1/4 tsp. | 1 mL |
| Pepper | 1/8 tsp. | 0.5 mL |
| Tomato pasta sauce | 2 cups | 500 mL |

Combine water and salt in Dutch oven. Bring to a boil. Add noodles. Boil, uncovered, for 12 to 15 minutes, stirring occasionally, until tender but firm. Drain. Rinse with cold water. Drain.

Heat cooking oil in medium frying pan on medium. Add mushrooms and onion. Cook for about 10 minutes, stirring occasionally, until liquid is evaporated. Transfer to large bowl.

Add next 5 ingredients. Stir. Arrange noodles on work surface. Spread about 1/3 cup (75 mL) cheese mixture along each noodle. Roll up jelly roll style from one end to enclose filling.

Spread 1/4 cup (60 mL) pasta sauce in bottom of greased 8 x 8 inch (20 x 20 cm) baking dish. Place rolls, seam-side down, over sauce. Pour remaining sauce over rolls. Cover with greased foil. Bake in 350°F (175°C) oven for about 45 minutes until heated through. Makes 8 roll-ups.

*1 roll-up: 272 Calories; 11.0 g Total Fat (0.7 g Mono, 0.3 g Poly, 5.5 g Sat); 29 mg Cholesterol; 27 g Carbohydrate; 5 g Fibre; 19 g Protein; 683 mg Sodium*

# Creamy Tomato Shiitake Rigatoni

*Fresh shiitake mushrooms add a unique and delicious flavour to this rich tomato sauce. For a milder flavour, substitute white or brown mushrooms.*

| | | |
|---|---|---|
| Water | 12 cups | 3 L |
| Salt | 1 1/2 tsp. | 7 mL |
| Rigatoni pasta | 3 1/2 cups | 875 mL |
| Olive (or cooking) oil | 1 tbsp. | 15 mL |
| Sliced fresh shiitake mushrooms | 2 cups | 500 mL |
| Chopped green onion | 2/3 cup | 150 mL |
| Garlic cloves, minced | 3 | 3 |
| (or 3/4 tsp., 4 mL, powder) | | |
| Dry (or alcohol-free) white wine | 1/3 cup | 75 mL |
| Can of tomato sauce | 14 oz. | 398 mL |
| Chopped fresh parsley | 1/4 cup | 60 mL |
| Granulated sugar | 2 tsp. | 10 mL |
| Half-and-half cream | 3/4 cup | 175 mL |
| Grated Romano cheese | 1/4 cup | 60 mL |

Combine water and salt in Dutch oven. Bring to a boil. Add pasta. Boil, uncovered, for 14 to 16 minutes, stirring occasionally, until tender but firm. Drain. Return to same pot. Cover to keep warm.

Heat olive oil in large frying pan on medium. Add next 3 ingredients. Cook for 3 to 5 minutes until onion is softened.

Add wine. Cook for about 3 minutes until liquid is evaporated.

Add next 3 ingredients. Stir. Reduce heat to medium-low. Simmer for about 5 minutes to blend flavours.

Add cream. Stir. Add to pasta. Toss.

Sprinkle with cheese. Makes about 6 cups (1.5 L).

*1 cup (250 mL): 276 Calories; 8.0 g Total Fat (2.7 g Mono, 0.5 g Poly, 3.5 g Sat); 16 mg Cholesterol; 40 g Carbohydrate; 2 g Fibre; 9 g Protein; 469 mg Sodium*

Pictured on page 90.

# Three-Cheese Spaghetti Pie

*This crispy and cheesy delight is sure to be a hit. Perfect served for brunch or dinner along with a salad or soup.*

| | | |
|---|---|---|
| Water | 12 cups | 3 L |
| Salt | 1 1/2 tsp. | 7 mL |
| Spaghetti, broken into thirds | 8 oz. | 225 g |
| Butter | 2 tbsp. | 30 mL |
| Large eggs, fork-beaten | 4 | 4 |
| Ricotta cheese | 1 cup | 250 mL |
| Milk | 1/2 cup | 125 mL |
| Thinly sliced roasted red peppers | 1/2 cup | 125 mL |
| Sliced green onion | 1/4 cup | 60 mL |
| Salt | 1/2 tsp. | 2 mL |
| Grated mozzarella cheese | 1/2 cup | 125 mL |
| Grated Parmesan cheese | 1/4 cup | 60 mL |

Combine water and salt in Dutch oven. Bring to a boil. Add pasta. Boil, uncovered, for 10 to 12 minutes, stirring occasionally, until tender but firm. Drain. Return to same pot. Add butter. Toss.

Combine next 6 ingredients in small bowl. Add to pasta. Toss until combined. Spread evenly in greased, deep-dish 9 inch (22 cm) pie plate. Bake, uncovered, in 350°F (175°C) oven for about 40 minutes until just set.

Sprinkle with mozzarella and Parmesan cheese. Bake for about 5 minutes until cheese is bubbly. Let stand for 10 minutes. Cuts into 6 wedges.

*1 wedge: 359 Calories; 14.3 g Total Fat (1.1 g Mono, 0.1 g Poly, 7.9 g Sat); 178 mg Cholesterol; 34 g Carbohydrate; 1 g Fibre; 20 g Protein; 689 mg Sodium*

## Paré Pointer

*Nobody's nose can be more than eleven inches long. One more inch and it would be a foot.*

Meatless

# Fresh Tomato Spinach Pasta

*Don't be afraid to get fresh with your food! Fresh tomatoes and spinach are tossed with salty feta and angel hair pasta for a flavourful, light entree.*

| | | |
|---|---|---|
| Water | 12 cups | 3 L |
| Salt | 1 1/2 tsp. | 7 mL |
| Angel hair pasta, broken in half | 8 oz. | 225 g |
| Olive (or cooking) oil | 1 tbsp. | 15 mL |
| Large tomatoes, diced | 4 | 4 |
| Garlic cloves, minced | 3 | 3 |
| (or 3/4 tsp., 4 mL, powder) | | |
| Fresh spinach leaves, lightly packed, coarsely chopped | 3 cups | 750 mL |
| Prepared vegetable broth | 1/3 cup | 75 mL |
| Dried marjoram | 1 tbsp. | 15 mL |
| Salt | 1/2 tsp. | 2 mL |
| Pepper | 1/2 tsp. | 2 mL |
| Crumbled feta cheese | 1/2 cup | 125 mL |

Combine water and salt in large saucepan. Bring to a boil. Add pasta. Boil, uncovered, for 3 to 5 minutes, stirring occasionally, until tender but firm. Drain. Return to same pot. Cover to keep warm.

Heat olive oil in large frying pan on medium. Add tomato and garlic. Heat and stir for about 3 minutes until fragrant. Add to pasta. Cover to keep warm.

Add next 5 ingredients to same frying pan. Heat on medium for 3 to 5 minutes, stirring occasionally, until spinach is wilted. Add to pasta mixture. Toss. Transfer to serving bowl.

Sprinkle with cheese. Makes about 6 cups (1.5 L).

*1 cup (250 mL): 223 Calories; 6.0 g Total Fat (2.3 g Mono, 0.6 g Poly, 2.3 g Sat); 11 mg Cholesterol; 34 g Carbohydrate; 3 g Fibre; 8 g Protein; 377 mg Sodium*

Pictured on page 89.

# Pepper And Kale Linguine

*This delicious and nutritious pasta is filled with colourful veggies in a sweet and tangy sauce.*

| | | |
|---|---|---|
| Water | 12 cups | 3 L |
| Salt | 1 1/2 tsp. | 7 mL |
| Whole-wheat linguine | 10 oz. | 285 g |
| Chopped kale leaves, lightly packed (see Tip, page 99) | 6 cups | 1.5 L |
| Olive (or cooking) oil | 1 tsp. | 5 mL |
| Thinly sliced onion | 1 cup | 250 mL |
| Garlic cloves, minced (or 1/2 tsp., 2 mL, powder) | 2 | 2 |
| Thinly sliced red pepper | 2 cups | 500 mL |
| Thinly sliced yellow pepper | 2 cups | 500 mL |
| Orange juice | 1/2 cup | 125 mL |
| Rice vinegar | 2 tbsp. | 30 mL |
| Soy sauce | 2 tbsp. | 30 mL |
| Ground ginger | 1 tsp. | 5 mL |
| Pepper | 1/4 tsp. | 1 mL |
| Water | 1 tbsp. | 15 mL |
| Cornstarch | 1 tbsp. | 15 mL |

Combine water and salt in Dutch oven. Bring to a boil. Add pasta. Boil, uncovered, for 7 minutes, stirring occasionally. Add kale. Stir. Cook, uncovered, for about 3 minutes until pasta is tender but firm and kale is tender. Drain, reserving 1/2 cup (125 mL) cooking water. Return pasta and kale to same pot. Cover to keep warm.

Heat olive oil in large frying pan on medium. Add onion and garlic. Cook for 5 to 10 minutes, stirring often, until onion is softened.

Add next 7 ingredients and reserved cooking water. Stir. Bring to a boil. Cook for about 3 minutes, stirring occasionally, until peppers are tender-crisp.

Stir water into cornstarch in small cup. Add to pan. Heat and stir for 1 to 2 minutes until boiling and slightly thickened. Add to pasta mixture. Toss. Makes about 8 cups (2 L).

*1 cup (250 mL): 197 Calories; 1.8 g Total Fat (0.5 g Mono, 0.4 g Poly, 0.3 g Sat); 0 mg Cholesterol; 39 g Carbohydrate; 4 g Fibre; 8 g Protein; 353 mg Sodium*

Pictured on page 89.

# Basil Garlic Spaghetti

*With summery sweet cherry tomatoes, fragrant basil and roasted garlic,*
*every bite is just bursting with flavour!*

| | | |
|---|---|---|
| Water | 12 cups | 3 L |
| Salt | 1 1/2 tsp. | 7 mL |
| Spaghetti | 12 oz. | 340 g |
| Cherry tomatoes | 3 cups | 750 mL |
| Kalamata olives | 1/4 cup | 60 mL |
| Garlic cloves, coarsely chopped | 6 | 6 |
| Salt | 1/2 tsp. | 2 mL |
| Coarsely ground pepper | 1/2 tsp. | 2 mL |
| Olive oil | 2 tbsp. | 30 mL |
| Bocconcini (or mozzarella), cut up (see Note) | 8 oz. | 225 g |
| Chopped fresh basil | 1/4 cup | 60 mL |

Combine water and salt in Dutch oven. Bring to a boil. Add pasta. Boil, uncovered, for 10 to 12 minutes, stirring occasionally, until tender but firm. Drain. Return to same pot. Cover to keep warm.

Combine next 5 ingredients in ungreased 9 x 13 inch (22 x 33 cm) baking dish.

Drizzle with olive oil. Toss. Bake, uncovered, in 425°F (220°C) oven for about 15 minutes, stirring occasionally, until garlic is softened.

Add bocconcini, basil and pasta to tomato mixture. Toss. Transfer to serving bowl. Makes about 7 1/2 cups (1.9 L).

*1 cup (250 mL): 297 Calories; 11.5 g Total Fat (3.1 g Mono, 0.7 g Poly, 2.8 g Sat); 11 mg Cholesterol; 38 g Carbohydrate; 3 g Fibre; 12 g Protein; 219 mg Sodium*

**Note:** Bocconcini is fresh mozzarella cheese.

 *tip* To remove the centre rib from lettuce or kale, fold the leaf in half along the rib and then cut along the length of the rib.

# Nutty Edamame Shells

*Edamame (pronounced eh-dah-MAH-meh) are young soybeans that are sold in the frozen section of your grocery store. They are available with or without the shell and are a great source of protein. Here they pair with pasta for the best meatless entree you could imagine.*

| | | |
|---|---|---|
| Water | 8 cups | 2 L |
| Salt | 1 tsp. | 5 mL |
| Small shell pasta | 3 cups | 750 mL |
| Frozen shelled edamame (soybeans) | 2 cups | 500 mL |
| Cooking oil | 1 tsp. | 5 mL |
| Chopped onion | 1 cup | 250 mL |
| Vegetable broth | 2 cups | 500 mL |
| Thai peanut sauce | 1/4 cup | 60 mL |
| Salt | 1/4 tsp. | 1 mL |
| Pepper, just a pinch | | |
| Frozen Oriental mixed vegetables | 2 cups | 500 mL |
| Water | 1 tbsp. | 15 mL |
| Cornstarch | 2 tsp. | 10 mL |

Combine water and salt in large saucepan. Bring to a boil. Add pasta. Boil, uncovered, for 6 minutes, stirring occasionally. Add edamame. Cook, uncovered, for 5 to 8 minutes, stirring occasionally, until pasta is tender but firm. Drain. Return to same pot. Cover to keep warm.

Heat cooking oil in large frying pan on medium. Add onion. Cook for 5 to 10 minutes, stirring often, until softened.

Add next 4 ingredients. Stir. Bring to a boil. Simmer for 5 minutes to blend flavours.

Add vegetables. Heat and stir for 3 to 5 minutes until vegetables are tender-crisp.

Stir water into cornstarch in small cup. Add to vegetable mixture. Heat and stir for 1 to 2 minutes until bubbling and thickened. Add to pasta mixture. Toss. Makes about 8 cups (2 L). Serves 4.

*1 cup (250 mL): 357 Calories; 9.1 g Total Fat (0.7 g Mono, 0.4 g Poly, 1.0 g Sat); 0 mg Cholesterol; 53 g Carbohydrate; 6 g Fibre; 16 g Protein; 691 mg Sodium*

Pictured on page 90.

# Bean-Stuffed Shells

*Looking for an elegant meatless main course? We've got you covered with these jumbo pasta shells filled with ricotta cheese and a white bean and pesto purée.*

| | | |
|---|---|---|
| Water | 12 cups | 3 L |
| Salt | 1 1/2 tsp. | 7 mL |
| Jumbo shell pasta | 24 | 24 |
| Tomato pasta sauce | 2 cups | 500 mL |
| Half-and-half cream | 1/2 cup | 125 mL |
| Fresh spinach leaves, lightly packed | 4 cups | 1 L |
| Can of navy beans, rinsed and drained | 19 oz. | 540 mL |
| Ricotta cheese | 1 cup | 250 mL |
| Basil pesto | 1 tbsp. | 15 mL |
| Grated lemon zest | 1 1/2 tsp. | 7 mL |
| Garlic powder | 1/2 tsp. | 2 mL |
| Salt | 1/2 tsp. | 2 mL |
| Pepper | 1/4 tsp. | 1 mL |
| Grated Parmesan cheese | 1 cup | 250 mL |

Combine water and salt in Dutch oven. Bring to a boil. Add pasta shells. Boil, uncovered, for 10 to 12 minutes, stirring occasionally, until tender but firm. Drain.

Combine pasta sauce and cream in small bowl. Spread 1 cup (250 mL) sauce mixture in bottom of greased 9 x 13 inch (22 x 33 cm) baking dish.

Put next 8 ingredients into food processor. Pulse with on/off motion until smooth. Spoon into large resealable freezer bag with piece snipped off corner. Pipe into pasta shells. Arrange in single layer over sauce mixture. Pour remaining sauce mixture over top.

Sprinkle with Parmesan cheese. Bake, covered, in 350°F (175°C) oven for 20 minutes until heated through and cheese is bubbling. Bake, uncovered, for another 20 minutes until cheese is browned. Makes 24 stuffed shells. Serves 4.

*1 serving: 657 Calories; 23.8 g Total Fat (1.1 g Mono, 0.4 g Poly, 13.1 g Sat); 67 mg Cholesterol; 74 g Carbohydrate; 11 g Fibre; 40 g Protein; 2145 mg Sodium*

Pictured on page 90.

# Farfalle Fagioli Y Fungi

*That's "bow ties, beans and mushrooms" to you! These tasty ingredients are even tastier tossed in a creamy tomato and Parmesan sauce.*

| | | |
|---|---|---|
| Water | 12 cups | 3 L |
| Salt | 1 1/2 tsp. | 7 mL |
| Medium bow pasta | 4 cups | 1 L |
| Can of romano (or pinto) beans, rinsed and drained | 19 oz. | 540 mL |
| Olive (or cooking) oil | 1 tbsp. | 15 mL |
| Sliced fresh brown (or white) mushrooms | 3 cups | 750 mL |
| Olive (or cooking) oil | 2 tsp. | 10 mL |
| Diced red pepper | 1 cup | 250 mL |
| Chopped onion | 1 cup | 250 mL |
| Garlic clove, minced (or 1/4 tsp., 1 mL, powder) | 1 | 1 |
| Can of diced tomatoes (with juice) | 19 oz. | 540 mL |
| Half-and-half cream | 1/2 cup | 125 mL |
| Grated Parmesan cheese | 1/3 cup | 75 mL |
| Salt | 1/2 tsp. | 2 mL |
| Pepper | 1/4 tsp. | 1 mL |

Combine water and salt in Dutch oven. Bring to a boil. Add pasta. Boil, uncovered, for 10 minutes, stirring occasionally. Add beans. Stir. Cook, uncovered, for about 2 minutes until pasta is tender but firm. Drain. Return to same pot. Cover to keep warm.

Heat first amount of olive oil in large saucepan on medium. Add mushrooms. Cook, uncovered, for 5 to 10 minutes, stirring often, until mushrooms are browned. Add to pasta mixture.

Reduce heat to medium. Heat second amount of olive oil in same pan. Add next 3 ingredients. Cook, uncovered, for 5 to 10 minutes, stirring occasionally, until onion is softened.

Add remaining 5 ingredients. Cook, uncovered, for about 5 minutes, stirring occasionally, to blend flavours. Carefully process with hand blender or in blender until smooth (see Note). Add to pasta mixture. Toss gently. Makes about 8 cups (2 L).

*(continued on next page)*

Meatless

*1 cup (250 mL): 312 Calories; 7.5 g Total Fat (2.6 g Mono, 1.0 g Poly, 2.5 g Sat); 11 mg Cholesterol; 49 g Carbohydrate; 6 g Fibre; 13 g Protein; 552 mg Sodium*

**Note:** Before processing hot liquids, check the operating instructions for your blender.

---

# Springtime Pasta

*Have a spring fling with this lovely pasta dish that evokes all the fresh flavours and textures of the season.*

| | | |
|---|---|---|
| Water | 12 cups | 3 L |
| Salt | 1 1/2 tsp. | 7 mL |
| Penne pasta | 3 cups | 750 mL |
| Olive oil | 2 tbsp. | 30 mL |
| Chopped fresh asparagus | 1 1/2 cups | 375 mL |
| Chopped green onion | 1/2 cup | 125 mL |
| Garlic cloves, minced | 2 | 2 |
| (or 1/2 tsp., 2 mL, powder) | | |
| Dried oregano | 1 1/2 tsp. | 7 mL |
| Fresh spinach leaves, lightly packed | 4 cups | 1 L |
| Frozen peas | 1 cup | 250 mL |
| Salt | 1/2 tsp. | 2 mL |
| Coarsely ground pepper | 1/4 tsp. | 1 mL |
| Grated Parmesan cheese | 1/2 cup | 125 mL |

Combine water and salt in Dutch oven. Bring to a boil. Add pasta. Boil, uncovered, for 14 to 16 minutes, stirring occasionally, until tender but firm. Drain, reserving 1/2 cup (125 mL) cooking water. Return pasta to same pot. Cover to keep warm.

Heat olive oil in large frying pan on medium. Add next 4 ingredients. Cook for about 5 minutes, stirring occasionally, until asparagus is tender-crisp.

Add next 4 ingredients. Cook for about 3 minutes, stirring occasionally, until spinach is wilted and peas are heated through. Add reserved pasta water. Stir. Add to pasta.

Sprinkle with cheese. Toss. Makes about 8 cups (2 L).

*1 cup (250 mL): 250 Calories; 6.7 g Total Fat (2.5 g Mono, 0.6 g Poly, 2.1 g Sat); 8 mg Cholesterol; 37 g Carbohydrate; 4 g Fibre; 11 g Protein; 317 mg Sodium*

Pictured on page 89.

Meatless

# Sensational Sesame Salad

*Create a dinnertime sensation with a salad of crisp cabbage and angel hair pasta tossed in a sweet honey-sesame dressing.*

| | | |
|---|---|---|
| Water | 8 cups | 2 L |
| Salt | 1 tsp. | 5 mL |
| Angel hair pasta, broken into thirds | 4 oz. | 113 g |
| Liquid honey | 2 tbsp. | 30 mL |
| Cooking oil | 1 tbsp. | 15 mL |
| Sesame oil (for flavour) | 1 tbsp. | 15 mL |
| Soy sauce | 1 tbsp. | 15 mL |
| Finely grated gingerroot | 1 1/2 tsp. | 7 mL |
| (or 1/2 tsp., 2 mL, ground ginger) | | |
| Dried crushed chilies | 1/2 tsp. | 2 mL |
| Coleslaw mix | 2 cups | 500 mL |
| Thinly sliced red pepper | 1/2 cup | 125 mL |
| Sliced green onion | 2 tbsp. | 30 mL |
| Sesame seeds, toasted (see Tip, below), for garnish | 1 tbsp. | 15 mL |

Combine water and salt in large saucepan. Bring to a boil. Add pasta. Boil, uncovered, for 3 to 5 minutes, stirring occasionally, until tender but firm. Drain. Rinse with cold water. Drain well.

Combine next 6 ingredients in large bowl.

Add next 3 ingredients and pasta. Toss.

Sprinkle with sesame seeds. Makes about 4 cups (1 L).

*1 cup (250 mL): 218 Calories; 7.7 g Total Fat (2.0 g Mono, 1.1 g Poly, 0.8 g Sat); 0 mg Cholesterol; 33 g Carbohydrate; 2 g Fibre; 4 g Protein; 343 mg Sodium*

 *tip* When toasting nuts, seeds or coconut, cooking times will vary for each type of nut—so never toast them together. For small amounts, place ingredient in an ungreased frying pan. Heat on medium for 3 to 5 minutes, stirring often, until golden. For larger amounts, spread ingredient evenly in an ungreased shallow pan. Bake in a 350°F (175°C) oven for 5 to 10 minutes, stirring or shaking often, until golden.

# Honey Lime Crab Salad

*This summery concoction of crabmeat, crisp veggies and creamy dressing is the perfect choice for your next family barbecue.*

| | | |
|---|---|---|
| Water | 8 cups | 2 L |
| Salt | 1 tsp. | 5 mL |
| Small shell pasta | 2 cups | 500 mL |
| Grated carrot | 1 cup | 250 mL |
| English cucumber (with peel), quartered lengthwise and sliced crosswise into 1/4 inch (6 mm) pieces | 1 cup | 250 mL |
| Cans of flaked crabmeat (4 1/4 oz., 120 g, each), drained, cartilage removed | 2 | 2 |
| Thinly sliced celery | 1/2 cup | 125 mL |
| Capers (optional) | 2 tbsp. | 30 mL |
| Mayonnaise | 1/2 cup | 125 mL |
| Lime juice | 1 tbsp. | 15 mL |
| Grated lime zest (see Tip, page 81) | 2 tsp. | 10 mL |
| Liquid honey | 1 tsp. | 5 mL |
| Ground cumin | 1/2 tsp. | 2 mL |
| Salt | 1/4 tsp. | 1 mL |
| Pepper | 1/4 tsp. | 1 mL |

Combine water and salt in large saucepan. Bring to a boil. Add pasta. Boil, uncovered, for 8 to 10 minutes, stirring occasionally, until tender but firm. Drain. Rinse with cold water. Drain. Transfer to medium bowl.

Add next 5 ingredients to pasta. Toss.

Combine remaining 7 ingredients in small bowl. Add to pasta mixture. Toss to coat. Makes about 6 cups (1.5 L).

*1 cup (250 mL): 264 Calories; 15.8 g Total Fat (0.1 g Mono, 0.2 g Poly, 2.1 g Sat); 42 mg Cholesterol; 19 g Carbohydrate; 1 g Fibre; 11 g Protein; 353 mg Sodium*

# Gazpacho Salad

*A cool soup becomes a cooler-than-cool pasta salad! The bright, refreshing flavours of tomato, cucumber and cilantro dress up radiatore pasta.*

| | | |
|---|---|---|
| Water | 8 cups | 2 L |
| Salt | 1 tsp. | 5 mL |
| Radiatore pasta | 2 cups | 500 mL |
| Can of diced tomatoes, drained | 14 oz. | 398 mL |
| Diced English cucumber (with peel) | 1 cup | 250 mL |
| Diced red pepper | 1 cup | 250 mL |
| Olive (or cooking) oil | 3 tbsp. | 50 mL |
| Red wine vinegar | 2 tbsp. | 30 mL |
| Chopped fresh basil (or 1 tsp., 5 mL, dried) | 4 tsp. | 20 mL |
| Lemon juice | 1 tbsp. | 15 mL |
| Liquid honey | 1 tbsp. | 15 mL |
| Chopped fresh cilantro | 2 tsp. | 10 mL |
| Ground cumin | 1/2 tsp. | 2 mL |
| Salt | 1/2 tsp. | 2 mL |
| Pepper | 1/4 tsp. | 1 mL |

Combine water and salt in large saucepan. Bring to a boil. Add pasta. Boil, uncovered, for 7 to 9 minutes, stirring occasionally, until tender but firm. Drain. Rinse with cold water. Drain well. Transfer to medium bowl.

Add next 3 ingredients. Toss.

Whisk remaining 9 ingredients in small bowl. Add to pasta mixture. Toss. Makes about 6 cups (1.5 L).

*1 cup (250 mL): 173 Calories; 7.5 g Total Fat (5.0 g Mono, 1.1 g Poly, 1.0 g Sat); 0 mg Cholesterol; 24 g Carbohydrate; 1 g Fibre; 4 g Protein; 375 mg Sodium*

Pictured at right.

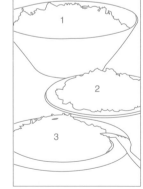

1. Chicken Caesar Pasta Salad, page 113
2. Gazpacho Salad, above
3. Salami Olive Penne Salad, page 110

Props courtesy of: Emile Henry

# Tuna Casserole Salad

*Too hot to bake? We've transformed the classic tuna casserole into a salad so you can enjoy it all year long. Try it with canned salmon as well.*

| | | |
|---|---|---|
| Water | 8 cups | 2 L |
| Salt | 1 tsp. | 5 mL |
| Small shell pasta | 1 1/2 cups | 375 mL |
| Frozen peas, thawed | 1 cup | 250 mL |
| Can of flaked white tuna, drained | 6 oz. | 170 g |
| Thinly sliced celery | 1/2 cup | 125 mL |
| Diced red pepper | 1/4 cup | 60 mL |
| Mayonnaise | 1/2 cup | 125 mL |
| Tangy dill relish | 3 tbsp. | 50 mL |
| Dijon mustard | 2 tsp. | 10 mL |
| Lemon pepper | 1/2 tsp. | 2 mL |
| Salt | 1/4 tsp. | 1 mL |

Paprika, sprinkle

Combine water and salt in large saucepan. Bring to a boil. Add pasta. Boil, uncovered, for 8 to 10 minutes, stirring occasionally, until tender but firm. Drain. Rinse with cold water. Drain well. Transfer to medium bowl.

Add next 4 ingredients. Toss.

Combine next 5 ingredients in small bowl. Add to pasta mixture. Stir to coat.

Sprinkle with paprika. Makes about 3 1/2 cups (875 mL).

*1 cup (250 mL): 450 Calories; 27.7 g Total Fat (0.4 g Mono, 0.6 g Poly, 3.9 g Sat); 32 mg Cholesterol; 32 g Carbohydrate; 4 g Fibre; 18 g Protein; 793 mg Sodium*

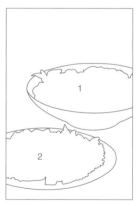

**SALMON CASSEROLE SALAD:** Omit tuna. Add canned salmon, round bones and skin removed.

1. Greek Rotini Salad, page 112
2. Fennel Avocado Salad, page 111

# Salami Olive Penne Salad

*Put a uniquely Italian spin on pasta salad with spicy salami, black olives
and a light dressing of tangy lemon and herbs.*

| | | |
|---|---|---|
| Water | 8 cups | 2 L |
| Salt | 1 tsp. | 5 mL |
| Penne pasta | 1 2/3 cups | 400 mL |
| Can of sliced black olives, drained | 4 1/2 oz. | 125 mL |
| Thinly sliced red onion | 1/3 cup | 75 mL |
| Thinly sliced salami, cut into strips | 2 oz. | 57 g |
| Finely shredded basil | 2 tbsp. | 30 mL |
| Lemon juice | 2 tbsp. | 30 mL |
| Olive (or cooking) oil | 2 tbsp. | 30 mL |
| Dried oregano | 2 tsp. | 10 mL |
| Dijon mustard | 1 tsp. | 5 mL |
| Granulated sugar | 1 tsp. | 5 mL |
| Lemon zest | 1 tsp. | 5 mL |
| Garlic cloves, minced | 1 | 1 |
|    (or 1/4 tsp., 1 mL, powder) | | |
| Salt | 1/8 tsp. | 0.5 mL |
| Pepper | 1/8 tsp. | 0.5 mL |
| Grated Parmesan cheese | 2 tbsp. | 30 mL |

Combine water and salt in large saucepan. Bring to a boil. Add pasta. Boil,
uncovered, for 14 to 16 minutes, stirring occasionally, until tender but firm.
Drain. Rinse with cold water. Drain. Transfer to medium bowl.

Add next 4 ingredients. Toss.

Whisk next 9 ingredients in small bowl. Add to pasta mixture. Toss.

Sprinkle with cheese. Toss. Makes about 4 cups (1 L).

*1 cup (250 mL): 375 Calories; 18.5 g Total Fat (7.5 g Mono, 1.3 g Poly, 5.0 g Sat);
31 mg Cholesterol; 41 g Carbohydrate; 3 g Fibre; 11 g Protein; 628 mg Sodium*

Pictured on page 107.

# Fennel Avocado Salad

*Simplicity itself! The flavours of avocado and fennel pair for a simple, yet delicious, combination.*

| | | |
|---|---|---|
| Water | 8 cups | 2 L |
| Salt | 1 tsp. | 5 mL |
| Medium bow pasta | 2 cups | 500 mL |
| Large ripe avocado, cut into 1/2 inch (12 mm) cubes | 1 | 1 |
| Crumbled feta cheese | 1/3 cup | 75 mL |
| Chopped pitted black olives | 1/4 cup | 60 mL |
| Olive (or cooking) oil | 3 tbsp. | 50 mL |
| Red wine vinegar | 2 tbsp. | 30 mL |
| Lemon juice | 1 tbsp. | 15 mL |
| Dried oregano | 1 tsp. | 5 mL |
| Salt | 1/4 tsp. | 1 mL |
| Pepper | 1/4 tsp. | 1 mL |
| Olive (or cooking) oil | 1 tsp. | 5 mL |
| Chopped fennel bulb (white part only) | 1 cup | 250 mL |
| Garlic cloves, minced (or 1/2 tsp., 2 mL, powder) | 2 | 2 |

Bring water and salt to a boil in large saucepan. Add pasta. Boil, uncovered, for 10 to 12 minutes, stirring occasionally, until tender but firm. Drain. Rinse with cold water. Drain. Transfer to large bowl.

Add next 3 ingredients. Toss.

Combine next 6 ingredients in small bowl. Add to pasta mixture. Toss.

Heat olive oil in small frying pan on medium. Add fennel and garlic. Cook for 5 to 10 minutes, stirring occasionally, until fennel is softened. Transfer to plate. Let stand for 5 minutes. Add to pasta mixture. Toss. Makes about 4 cups (1 L).

*1 cup (250 mL): 395 Calories; 23.4 g Total Fat (14.5 g Mono, 2.8 g Poly, 4.7 g Sat); 11 mg Cholesterol; 40 g Carbohydrate; 6 g Fibre; 9 g Protein; 373 mg Sodium*

Pictured on page 108.

# Greek Rotini Salad

*We love the fresh veggies, tangy olives and feta of a classic Greek salad—but who knew it'd be even better with pasta?*

| | | |
|---|---|---|
| Cooked rotini pasta | 3 cups | 750 mL |
| (about 1 1/2 cups, 375 mL, uncooked) | | |
| Diced English cucumber (with peel) | 1 cup | 250 mL |
| Grape tomatoes, halved | 20 | 20 |
| Chopped green pepper | 1/2 cup | 125 mL |
| Chopped red onion | 1/2 cup | 125 mL |
| Chopped red pepper | 1/2 cup | 125 mL |
| Whole pitted kalamata olives | 1/4 cup | 60 mL |
| Olive oil | 1/3 cup | 75 mL |
| Lemon juice | 3 tbsp. | 50 mL |
| Chopped fresh parsley | 2 tbsp. | 30 mL |
| (or 1 1/2 tsp., 7 mL, flakes) | | |
| Chopped fresh oregano | 1 tsp. | 5 mL |
| (or 1/4 tsp., 1 mL, dried) | | |
| Garlic clove, minced | 1 | 1 |
| (or 1/4 tsp., 1 mL, powder) | | |
| Salt | 1/4 tsp. | 1 mL |
| Pepper | 1/8 tsp. | 0.5 mL |
| Crumbled feta cheese | 3/4 cup | 175 mL |

Combine first 7 ingredients in large bowl.

Combine next 7 ingredients in jar with tight-fitting lid. Shake well. Drizzle over pasta mixture. Toss.

Sprinkle with cheese. Makes about 6 cups (1.5 L).

*1 cup (250 mL): 243 Calories; 17.5 g Total Fat (10.2 g Mono, 2.1 g Poly, 4.7 g Sat); 17 mg Cholesterol; 18 g Carbohydrate; 2 g Fibre; 6 g Protein; 360 mg Sodium*

Pictured on page 108.

# Chicken Caesar Pasta Salad

*That's right—even this classic salad can be improved with the addition of pasta! We've also added pesto-roasted chicken to the mix for even more flavour.*

| Ingredient | Imperial | Metric |
|---|---|---|
| Water | 8 cups | 2 L |
| Salt | 1 tsp. | 5 mL |
| Radiatore pasta | 2 cups | 500 mL |
| Romaine lettuce mix, lightly packed | 6 cups | 1.5 L |
| Boneless, skinless chicken breast halves | 3/4 lb. | 340 g |
| Basil pesto | 2 tbsp. | 30 mL |
| Caesar dressing | 2/3 cup | 150 mL |
| Lemon juice | 1 tbsp. | 15 mL |
| Coarsely ground pepper | 1 tsp. | 5 mL |
| Grated lemon zest | 1 tsp. | 5 mL |
| Grated Parmesan cheese | 1/4 cup | 60 mL |
| Bacon bits | 2 tbsp. | 30 mL |

Combine water and salt in large saucepan. Bring to a boil. Add pasta. Boil, uncovered, for 7 to 9 minutes, stirring occasionally, until tender but firm. Drain. Rinse with cold water. Drain well. Transfer to extra-large bowl.

Add lettuce mix. Toss.

Place chicken breasts on greased baking sheet. Brush with pesto. Broil for about 10 minutes, turning once at halftime, until fully cooked and internal temperature reaches 170°F (77°C). Remove to large plate. Cool. Cut into 1 inch (2.5 cm) cubes. Add to pasta mixture.

Whisk next 4 ingredients in small bowl. Add to pasta mixture. Toss.

Sprinkle with cheese and bacon. Makes about 10 cups (2.5 L).

*1 cup (250 mL): 216 Calories; 12.5 g Total Fat (2.4 g Mono, 5.3 g Poly, 2.5 g Sat); 25 mg Cholesterol; 13 g Carbohydrate; 1 g Fibre; 12.5 g Protein; 316 mg Sodium*

Pictured on page 107.

# Pear And Shrimp Salad

*This colourful pasta salad is packed with shrimp, sweet pears and red pepper.*
*A tangy vinaigrette completes this refreshing dish.*

| | | |
|---|---|---|
| Cooked rotini pasta | 3 cups | 750 mL |
| (about 1 1/2 cups, 375 mL, uncooked) | | |
| Cooked salad shrimp | 2 cups | 500 mL |
| Chopped peeled pears | 1 1/2 cups | 375 mL |
| Chopped red pepper | 1 cup | 250 mL |
| Olive (or cooking) oil | 3 tbsp. | 50 mL |
| White wine vinegar | 2 tbsp. | 30 mL |
| Liquid honey | 1 tbsp. | 15 mL |
| Chopped fresh cilantro | 2 tsp. | 10 mL |
| Dijon mustard | 2 tsp. | 10 mL |
| Ground ginger | 1/2 tsp. | 2 mL |
| Salt | 1/2 tsp. | 2 mL |
| Pepper | 1/4 tsp. | 1 mL |

Combine first 4 ingredients in large bowl.

Whisk remaining 8 ingredients in small bowl. Add to pasta mixture. Toss. Makes about 6 cups (1.5 L).

*1 cup (250 mL): 260 Calories; 13.1 g Total Fat (6.5 g Mono, 3.9 g Poly, 1.9 g Sat); 69 mg Cholesterol; 25 g Carbohydrate; 3 g Fibre; 12 g Protein; 347 mg Sodium*

# Nuts About Noodles

*Walnuts and blue cheese are a classic combination. Sometimes gourmet*
*flavours come from such simple ingredients!*

| | | |
|---|---|---|
| Water | 8 cups | 2 L |
| Salt | 1 tsp. | 5 mL |
| Radiatore pasta | 3 1/2 cups | 875 mL |
| Cooked salad shrimp | 1 1/2 cups | 375 mL |
| Chopped walnuts, toasted | 1 cup | 250 mL |
| (see Tip, page 104) | | |
| Blue cheese dressing | 1/2 cup | 125 mL |
| Sliced green onion | 1/4 cup | 60 mL |
| Pepper | 1/4 tsp. | 1 mL |

*(continued on next page)*

**114** Salads

Combine water and salt in large saucepan. Bring to a boil. Add pasta. Boil, uncovered, for 7 to 9 minutes, stirring occasionally, until tender but firm. Drain. Rinse with cold water. Drain.

Combine remaining 5 ingredients in large bowl. Add pasta. Toss. Makes about 6 cups (1.5 L).

*1 cup (250 mL): 455 Calories; 28.6 g Total Fat (5.4 g Mono, 17.2 g Poly, 3.9 g Sat); 55 mg Cholesterol; 36 g Carbohydrate; 3 g Fibre; 16 g Protein; 321 mg Sodium*

---

# Mango Chicken Salad

*This tangy pasta salad with bursts of fresh, sweet mango is sure to give you all the energy you need.*

| | | |
|---|---|---|
| Chopped cooked chicken | 2 cups | 500 mL |
| Cooked rigatoni pasta | 2 cups | 500 mL |
| (about 1 cup, 250 mL, uncooked) | | |
| Frozen, thawed mango, larger pieces | 1 1/2 cups | 375 mL |
| chopped | | |
| Thinly sliced celery | 1 1/2 cups | 375 mL |
| Sour cream | 1/2 cup | 125 mL |
| Finely chopped pickled jalapeño pepper | 1 tbsp. | 15 mL |
| Liquid honey | 1 tbsp. | 15 mL |
| Grated lime zest | 1 tsp. | 5 mL |
| Ground cumin | 1/2 tsp. | 2 mL |
| Garlic powder | 1/4 tsp. | 1 mL |
| Salt | 1/2 tsp. | 2 mL |
| Pepper | 1/4 tsp. | 1 mL |

Combine first 4 ingredients in medium bowl.

Combine remaining 8 ingredients in small bowl. Add to pasta mixture. Toss to coat. Makes about 6 cups (1.5 L).

*1 cup (250 mL): 230 Calories; 7.5 g Total Fat (1.2 g Mono, 0.8 g Poly, 3.2 g Sat); 55 mg Cholesterol; 23 g Carbohydrate; 2 g Fibre; 17 g Protein; 402 mg Sodium*

# Chipotle Cream Sauce

*This sauce brings together a wide range of flavours. There's spicy and smoky chipotle, rich cream and tangy orange. Works well with any pasta.*

| | | |
|---|---|---|
| Cooking oil | 1 tsp. | 5 mL |
| Chopped onion | 1 cup | 250 mL |
| Finely chopped chipotle peppers in adobo sauce (see Tip, below) | 1 tbsp. | 15 mL |
| Garlic cloves, minced (or 1/2 tsp., 2 mL, powder) | 2 | 2 |
| Granulated sugar | 1 tsp. | 5 mL |
| Ground cumin | 1 tsp. | 5 mL |
| Ground ginger | 1 tsp. | 5 mL |
| Salt | 1/2 tsp. | 2 mL |
| Pepper | 1/4 tsp. | 1 mL |
| All-purpose flour | 1 tbsp. | 15 mL |
| Can of diced tomatoes (with juice) | 28 oz. | 796 mL |
| Chopped roasted red pepper | 1/2 cup | 125 mL |
| Orange juice | 1/3 cup | 75 mL |
| Whipping cream | 1 cup | 250 mL |

Heat cooking oil in medium saucepan on medium. Add next 8 ingredients. Cook, uncovered, for 5 to 10 minutes, stirring often, until onion is softened.

Add flour. Heat and stir for 1 minute.

Add next 3 ingredients. Heat and stir until boiling and thickened. Carefully process with hand blender or in blender until smooth (see Note).

Add cream. Stir. Store in airtight container in refrigerator for up to 3 days or in freezer for up to 1 month. Makes about 5 1/2 cups (1.4 L).

*1 cup (250 mL): 132 Calories; 4.0 g Total Fat (0.5 g Mono, 0.3 g Poly, 2.3 g Sat); 15 mg Cholesterol; 20 g Carbohydrate; 1 g Fibre; 3 g Protein; 826 mg Sodium*

Pictured on page 126.

**Note:** Before processing hot liquids, check the operating instructions for your blender.

 *tip* Chipotle chili peppers are smoked jalapeño peppers. Be sure to wash your hands after handling. To store any leftover chipotle chili peppers, divide into recipe-friendly portions and freeze, with sauce, in airtight containers for up to one year.

# Red Clam Sauce

*This rich and hearty sauce is sure to impress. With flavours reminiscent of a Manhattan clam chowder, it'll go great with any type of pasta.*

| | | |
|---|---|---|
| Cooking oil | 1 tbsp. | 15 mL |
| Chopped celery | 1 cup | 250 mL |
| Chopped green pepper | 1 cup | 250 mL |
| Chopped onion | 1 cup | 250 mL |
| Garlic cloves, minced (or 1/2 tsp., 2 mL, powder) | 2 | 2 |
| Dry (or alcohol-free) red wine | 1/2 cup | 125 mL |
| Cans of tomato sauce (14 oz., 398 mL, each) | 2 | 2 |
| Reserved juice from clams | 1 1/2 cups | 375 mL |
| Tomato paste (see Tip, page 121) | 2 tbsp. | 30 mL |
| Italian seasoning | 1 tbsp. | 15 mL |
| Pepper | 1/4 tsp. | 1 mL |
| Salt | 1/4 tsp. | 1 mL |
| Cans of whole baby clams (5 oz., 142 g, each), drained and juice reserved | 2 | 2 |
| Chopped fresh parsley | 2 tbsp. | 30 mL |

Heat cooking oil in large frying pan on medium. Add next 4 ingredients. Cook for 5 to 10 minutes, stirring occasionally, until onion is softened.

Add wine. Heat and stir for 1 minute.

Add next 6 ingredients. Stir. Bring to a boil. Reduce heat to medium-low. Simmer, partially covered, for 15 minutes to blend flavours.

Add clams and parsley. Stir. Store in airtight container in refrigerator for up to 3 days or in freezer for up to 1 month. Makes about 7 cups (1.75 L).

*1 cup (250 mL): 132 Calories; 3.3 g Total Fat (1.2 g Mono, 0.6 g Poly, 0.6 g Sat); 32 mg Cholesterol; 15 g Carbohydrate; 2 g Fibre; 9 g Protein; 946 mg Sodium*

# Cajun Seafood Sauce

*Bring some Cajun flair to your dinner table with this mildly spicy sauce filled with seafood. Serve over your favourite pasta.*

| | | |
|---|---|---|
| Cooking oil | 2 tsp. | 10 mL |
| Chopped onion | 1 cup | 250 mL |
| Garlic clove, minced | 1 | 1 |
| (or 1/4 tsp., 1 mL, powder) | | |
| | | |
| Diced green pepper | 1/2 cup | 125 mL |
| Diced celery | 1/4 cup | 60 mL |
| Cajun seasoning | 1 tbsp. | 15 mL |
| Dried thyme | 1/2 tsp. | 2 mL |
| Bay leaf (see Note) | 1 | 1 |
| | | |
| Can of diced tomatoes (with juice) | 14 oz. | 398 mL |
| Clam tomato beverage | 1/2 cup | 125 mL |
| Dry (or alcohol-free) white wine | 1/4 cup | 60 mL |
| Granulated sugar | 1 tsp. | 5 mL |
| | | |
| Package of frozen mixed seafood, thawed | 12 oz. | 340 g |
| Cod fillets (or other white fish), any small | 1/2 lb. | 225 g |
| bones removed, cut into 1 inch | | |
| (2.5 cm) pieces | | |
| | | |
| Chopped fresh basil | 1 tbsp. | 15 mL |

Heat cooking oil in large saucepan on medium. Add onion and garlic. Cook, uncovered, for 5 to 10 minutes, stirring often, until onion is softened.

Add next 5 ingredients. Cook, uncovered, for 3 to 5 minutes, stirring occasionally, until celery starts to soften.

Add next 4 ingredients. Stir. Bring to a boil. Simmer, covered, for about 5 minutes to blend flavours.

Add seafood mix and cod. Cook, covered, for 3 to 5 minutes, stirring once, until fish flakes easily when tested with a fork. Remove and discard bay leaf.

*(continued on next page)*

Add basil. Stir. Store in airtight container in refrigerator for up to 2 days. Makes about 5 cups (1.25 L).

*1 cup (250 mL): 147 Calories; 2.6 g Total Fat (1.2 g Mono, 0.9 g Poly, 0.3 g Sat); 106 mg Cholesterol; 12 g Carbohydrate; 1 g Fibre; 18 g Protein; 808 mg Sodium*

**Note:** While stirring, be careful not to break up the bay leaf.

# Big-Batch Tomato Sauce

*Make a batch of this versatile sauce ahead of time and freeze it in smaller portions for busy days. All you'll have to do is cook up some of your favourite pasta to serve it over. If you prefer a smooth sauce, process it in your blender.*

| | | |
|---|---|---|
| Cooking oil | 1 tbsp. | 15 mL |
| Chopped onion | 2 cups | 500 mL |
| Chopped celery | 1 cup | 250 mL |
| Italian seasoning | 4 tsp. | 20 mL |
| Garlic cloves, minced | 3 | 3 |
| (or 3/4 tsp., 4 mL, powder) | | |
| Dried crushed chilies | 1/4 tsp. | 1 mL |
| Bay leaves (see Note) | 2 | 2 |
| Can of diced tomatoes (with juice) | 28 oz. | 796 mL |
| Chopped green pepper | 2 cups | 500 mL |
| Can of crushed tomatoes | 14 oz. | 398 mL |
| Tomato paste (see Tip, page 121) | 1/4 cup | 60 mL |
| Ketchup | 2 tbsp. | 30 mL |
| Granulated sugar | 2 tsp. | 10 mL |

Heat cooking oil in Dutch oven on medium. Add next 6 ingredients. Cook, uncovered, for about 10 minutes, stirring occasionally, until onion is softened.

Add next 6 ingredients. Stir. Reduce heat to medium-low. Simmer, covered, for about 30 minutes to blend flavours. Store in airtight container in refrigerator for up to 1 week or in freezer for up to 6 months. Makes about 7 cups (1.75 L).

*1 cup (250 mL): 107 Calories; 2.2 g Total Fat (1.2 g Mono, 0.6 g Poly, 0.2 g Sat); 0 mg Cholesterol; 21 g Carbohydrate; 3 g Fibre; 3 g Protein; 453 mg Sodium*

**Note:** While stirring, be careful not to break up the bay leaf.

# Nutty Sage Sauce

*Looking for a new sauce to add personality to your lasagna? Try this rich, creamy sauce with the warm, toasty flavours of sage and pecans. It's excellent over just about any other pasta, too!*

| | | |
|---|---|---|
| Butter (or hard margarine) | 1 tbsp. | 15 mL |
| Finely chopped onion | 1 cup | 250 mL |
| Garlic cloves, minced | 2 | 2 |
| (or 1/2 tsp., 2 mL, powder) | | |
| Coarsely chopped pecans, toasted | 1 cup | 250 mL |
| (see Tip, page 104) | | |
| Chopped fresh sage | 2 tbsp. | 30 mL |
| (or 1 1/2 tsp., 7 mL, dried) | | |
| Salt | 1/2 tsp. | 2 mL |
| Pepper | 1/4 tsp. | 1 mL |
| All-purpose flour | 1/4 cup | 60 mL |
| Half-and-half cream | 2 cups | 500 mL |
| Prepared vegetable broth | 1 cup | 250 mL |

Melt butter in medium saucepan on medium. Add onion and garlic. Cook, uncovered, for about 5 to 10 minutes, stirring often, until onion is softened.

Add next 4 ingredients. Heat and stir for 1 minute.

Add flour. Heat and stir for 1 minute. Slowly add cream and broth, stirring constantly, until smooth. Heat and stir for 5 to 10 minutes until boiling and thickened. Store in airtight container in refrigerator for up to 3 days or in freezer for up to 1 month. Makes about 3 cups (750 mL).

*1/2 cup (125 mL): 293 Calories; 25.5 g Total Fat (11.2 g Mono, 4.7 g Poly, 8.2 g Sat); 35 mg Cholesterol; 14 g Carbohydrate; 3 g Fibre; 5 g Protein; 318 mg Sodium*

# Chipotle Meatball Sauce

*Sure, you could spend an hour rolling meatballs, but who are we kidding?*
*The ready-made ones work just as well when you haven't got that kind of*
*time. This thick tomato slow cooker sauce has a great smoky, chipotle heat.*

| | | |
|---|---|---|
| Chopped onion | 2 cups | 500 mL |
| Box of frozen cooked meatballs, thawed | 2 1/4 lbs. | 1 kg |
| Can of crushed tomatoes | 28 oz. | 796 mL |
| Can of diced tomatoes (with juice) | 28 oz. | 796 mL |
| Chopped roasted red peppers, rinsed and drained | 1 cup | 250 mL |
| Tomato paste (see Tip, below) | 3 tbsp. | 50 mL |
| Chili powder | 1 tbsp. | 15 mL |
| Finely chopped chipotle peppers in adobo sauce (see Tip, page 116) | 1 tbsp. | 15 mL |
| Granulated sugar | 2 tsp. | 10 mL |
| Garlic powder | 3/4 tsp. | 4 mL |
| Salt | 1/2 tsp. | 2 mL |

Put onion into bottom of 5 to 6 quart (5 to 6 L) slow cooker.
Add meatballs.

Combine remaining 9 ingredients in medium bowl. Pour over meatballs.
Do not stir. Cook, covered, on Low for 8 to 9 hours or on High for 4 to
4 1/2 hours. Store in airtight container in refrigerator for up to 5 days or in
freezer for up to 3 months. Makes about 12 cups (3 L).

**1 cup (250 mL):** *200 Calories; 6.3 g Total Fat (0 g Mono, trace Poly, 2.9 g Sat); 16 mg Cholesterol;*
*25 g Carbohydrate; 2 g Fibre; 9 g Protein; 823 mg Sodium*

 *tip*    If a recipe calls for less than an entire can of tomato paste,
freeze the unopened can for 30 minutes. Open both ends and
push the contents through one end. Slice off only what you need.
Freeze the remaining paste in a resealable freezer bag or plastic
wrap for future use.

# Sassy Sauce

*The name says it all! Red wine and spicy Italian sausage add a ton of sass to the gentle sweetness of squash. Serve this slow cooker sauce with multi-coloured fettuccine for a truly stylish supper.*

| | | |
|---|---|---|
| Cooking oil | 2 tsp. | 10 mL |
| Italian sausage, casing removed | 1 1/2 lb. | 680 g |
| Garlic cloves, minced | 2 | 2 |
| (or 1/2 tsp., 2 mL, powder) | | |
| Can of crushed tomatoes | 28 oz. | 796 mL |
| Chopped butternut squash | 2 1/2 cups | 625 mL |
| Chopped celery | 2 cups | 500 mL |
| Chopped onion | 2 cups | 500 mL |
| Can of tomato sauce | 14 oz. | 398 mL |
| Dry (or alcohol-free) red wine | 1 cup | 250 mL |
| Dried oregano | 1 tsp. | 5 mL |
| Dried basil | 1/2 tsp. | 2 mL |
| Bay leaf | 1 | 1 |
| Salt | 1/4 tsp. | 1 mL |
| Pepper | 1/2 tsp. | 2 mL |

Heat cooking oil in large frying pan on medium-high. Add sausage and garlic. Scramble-fry for about 5 minutes until browned. Drain. Transfer to 4 to 5 quart (4 to 5 L) slow cooker.

Add remaining 11 ingredients. Stir. Cook, covered, on Low for 8 to 10 hours or on High for 4 to 5 hours. Remove and discard bay leaf. Store in airtight container in refrigerator for up to 5 days or in freezer for up to 3 months. Makes about 9 cups (2.25 L).

*1 cup (250 mL): 258 Calories; 11.7 g Total Fat (5.2 g Mono, 1.6 g Poly, 3.8 g Sat); 22 mg Cholesterol; 24 g Carbohydrate; 4 g Fibre; 11 g Protein; 939 mg Sodium*

Pictured on page 126.

# Creamy Tuscan Tomato Sauce

*Evoke the robust flavours of Tuscany on your next plate of pasta! This*
*luscious sauce is good with both short and long pasta.*

| | | |
|---|---|---|
| Olive (or cooking) oil | 1 tbsp. | 15 mL |
| Chopped onion | 1 cup | 250 mL |
| Garlic cloves, minced | 2 | 2 |
| (or 1/2 tsp., 2 mL, powder) | | |
| Dry (or alcohol-free) white wine | 1/2 cup | 125 mL |
| Lemon juice | 2 tbsp. | 30 mL |
| Can of diced tomatoes, drained | 28 oz. | 796 mL |
| Whipping cream | 1/2 cup | 125 mL |
| Chopped pitted kalamata olives | 1/3 cup | 75 mL |
| Salt, just a pinch | | |
| Pepper, just a pinch | | |
| Capers (optional) | 2 tbsp. | 30 mL |

Heat olive oil in large frying pan on medium. Add onion and garlic. Cook for 5 to 10 minutes, stirring often, until onion is softened.

Add wine and lemon juice. Bring to a boil. Simmer for about 2 minutes until reduced by half. Add tomatoes. Stir. Bring to a boil. Simmer, stirring occasionally, for about 15 minutes until thickened.

Add remaining 5 ingredients. Heat and stir for about 2 minutes to blend flavours. Store in airtight container in refrigerator for up to 3 days or in freezer for up to 1 month. Makes about 4 cups (1 L).

*1 cup (250 mL): 158 Calories; 6.7 g Total Fat (3.4 g Mono, 0.6 g Poly, 2.2 g Sat); 10 mg Cholesterol; 15 g Carbohydrate; 2 g Fibre; 2 g Protein; 565 mg Sodium*

## Paré Pointer
*That bird is always out of breath—he's a puffin.*

# Thai Curry Sauce

*Thai red curry paste, coconut and lime come together for a flavourful combination—but don't be scared away; this sauce is only mildly spicy. Serve over angel hair or vermicelli.*

| | | |
|---|---|---|
| Cooking oil | 1 tsp. | 5 mL |
| Chopped fresh white mushrooms | 3 cups | 750 mL |
| Chopped onion | 1 cup | 250 mL |
| Chopped red pepper | 1 cup | 250 mL |
| Can of bamboo shoots, drained and chopped | 8 oz. | 227 mL |
| Garlic powder | 1/2 tsp. | 2 mL |
| Ground ginger | 1/2 tsp. | 2 mL |
| Red curry paste | 1/2 tsp. | 2 mL |
| Salt | 1/2 tsp. | 2 mL |
| Pepper | 1/4 tsp. | 1 mL |
| Can of coconut milk | 14 oz. | 398 mL |
| Lime juice | 1 tsp. | 5 mL |

Heat cooking oil in large saucepan on medium. Add mushrooms and onion. Cook, uncovered, for about 10 minutes, stirring occasionally, until onion is softened.

Add next 7 ingredients. Cook, uncovered, for about 5 minutes, stirring occasionally, until red pepper starts to soften.

Add coconut milk. Heat and stir for 1 to 2 minutes until heated through. Add lime juice. Stir. Store in airtight container in refrigerator for up to 3 days or in freezer for up to 1 month. Makes about 3 cups (750 mL).

*1/2 cup (125 mL): 169 Calories; 15.2 g Total Fat (1.1 g Mono, 0.4 g Poly, 12.6 g Sat); 0 mg Cholesterol; 9 g Carbohydrate; 2 g Fibre; 3 g Protein; 221 mg Sodium*

1. Green Pepper Sausage Sauce, page 135
2. Smoked Salmon Sauce, page 137
3. Roasted Pepper Chèvre Sauce, page 129

Props courtesy of: Anchor Hocking Canada

# Herb Cream Sauce

*Dried herbs? Not in this pasta sauce! You won't believe the difference that fresh herbs make in this thick, creamy wine-flavoured sauce. Serve with seafood or over your favourite pasta.*

| | | |
|---|---|---|
| Butter (or hard margarine) | 2 tbsp. | 30 mL |
| Finely chopped onion | 1/2 cup | 125 mL |
| Garlic cloves, minced | 2 | 2 |
| (or 1/2 tsp., 2 mL, powder) | | |
| All-purpose flour | 1/4 cup | 60 mL |
| Salt | 1 tsp. | 5 mL |
| Pepper | 1/4 tsp. | 1 mL |
| Half-and-half cream | 2 cups | 500 mL |
| Milk | 1 cup | 250 mL |
| Dry (or alcohol-free) white wine | 1/2 cup | 125 mL |
| Finely chopped fresh basil | 2 tbsp. | 30 mL |
| Finely chopped fresh oregano | 1 tbsp. | 15 mL |
| Finely chopped fresh parsley | 1 tbsp. | 15 mL |

Melt butter in medium saucepan on medium. Add onion and garlic. Cook, uncovered, for about 5 minutes, stirring often, until onion is softened.

Add next 3 ingredients. Heat and stir for 2 minutes.

Slowly add cream, stirring constantly until boiling and thickened. Remove from heat. Add remaining 5 ingredients. Stir. Store in airtight container in refrigerator for up to 3 days or in freezer for up to 1 month. Makes about 3 2/3 cups (900 mL).

*1/2 cup (125 mL): 158 Calories; 10.8 g Total Fat (3.1 g Mono, 0.4 g Poly, 6.7 g Sat); 34 mg Cholesterol; 9 g Carbohydrate; trace Fibre; 4 g Protein; 377 mg Sodium*

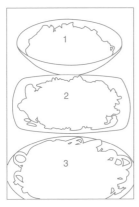

1. Sassy Sauce, page 122
2. Chipotle Cream Sauce, page 116
3. Parma Sauce, page 131

Props courtesy of: Pfaltzgraff Canada

# Tofu Pesto Sauce

*A rich, creamy sauce—without the cream! Tofu provides the smooth texture,*
*while pesto and balsamic vinegar add tons of flavour.*

| | | |
|---|---|---|
| Packages of soft tofu | 2 | 2 |
| (10 1/2 oz., 300 g, each) | | |
| Sun-dried tomato pesto | 1/4 cup | 60 mL |
| Olive oil | 1 tbsp. | 15 mL |
| Balsamic vinegar | 2 tsp. | 10 mL |
| Salt | 1/4 tsp. | 1 mL |
| Pepper | 1/4 tsp. | 1 mL |

Put all 6 ingredients into blender or food processor. Process until smooth.
Store in airtight container in refrigerator for up to 1 week. Makes about
3 cups (750 mL).

*1/2 cup (125 mL): 82 Calories; 5.0 g Total Fat (2.2 g Mono, 1.9 g Poly, 0.7 g Sat); 0 mg Cholesterol;*
*4 g Carbohydrate; trace Fibre; 5 g Protein; 207 mg Sodium*

# Fennel Orange Tomato Sauce

*Forget plain tomato sauce—this one's enhanced with the fresh flavours of*
*fennel and orange. A spiral pasta like fusilli or radiatore will "grab" the*
*sauce, ensuring that you don't waste a single drop!*

| | | |
|---|---|---|
| Olive (or cooking) oil | 2 tbsp. | 30 mL |
| Chopped fennel bulb (white part only) | 2 1/2 cups | 625 mL |
| Dried basil | 1 tsp. | 5 mL |
| Dried oregano | 1 tsp. | 5 mL |
| Garlic clove, minced | 1 | 1 |
| (or 1/4 tsp., 1 mL, powder) | | |
| Fennel seed, crushed | 1/2 tsp. | 2 mL |
| Dried crushed chilies | 1/8 tsp. | 0.5 mL |
| Can of diced tomatoes (with juice) | 28 oz. | 796 mL |
| Orange juice | 1/4 cup | 60 mL |
| Granulated sugar | 1 tbsp. | 15 mL |
| Grated orange zest | 1 tsp. | 5 mL |
| Salt | 1/2 tsp. | 2 mL |
| Pepper | 1/4 tsp. | 1 mL |

*(continued on next page)*

Heat olive oil in large saucepan on medium. Add fennel. Cook, uncovered, for about 10 minutes, stirring occasionally, until fennel starts to brown.

Add next 5 ingredients. Heat and stir for 1 minute until fragrant.

Add remaining 6 ingredients. Stir. Bring to a boil. Reduce heat to medium-low. Cook, uncovered, stirring occasionally, for about 15 minutes until fennel is tender. Carefully process with hand blender or in blender until smooth (see Note). Store in airtight container in refrigerator for up to 5 days, or in freezer for up to 6 months. Makes about 5 1/2 cups (1.4 L).

**1 cup (250 mL):** *97 Calories; 5.3 g Total Fat (3.6 g Mono, 0.8 g Poly, 0.7 g Sat); 0 mg Cholesterol; 13 g Carbohydrate; 2 g Fibre; 2 g Protein; 626 mg Sodium*

**Note:** Before processing hot liquids, check the operating instructions for your blender.

# Roasted Pepper Chèvre Sauce

*This versatile rosé-coloured sauce is great served over penne or rotini. It's also fabulous on pizza or with chicken or pork. For colour variation, substitute yellow peppers for the red.*

| | | |
|---|---|---|
| Unpeeled garlic cloves | 4 | 4 |
| Large red peppers | 5 | 5 |
| Soft goat (chèvre) cheese | 1/2 cup | 125 mL |
| Salt | 1/2 tsp. | 2 mL |
| Pepper | 1/4 tsp. | 1 mL |

Wrap garlic in foil. Arrange garlic and red peppers on greased baking sheet. Bake in 400°F (205°C) oven for about 40 minutes until garlic and peppers are tender. Unwrap garlic. Put garlic and peppers into large bowl. Let stand, covered, for 10 minutes. Remove and discard skin, stems and seeds from peppers. Coarsely chop. Transfer to food processor or blender along with any juices from bowl. Peel garlic. Add to peppers. Process until smooth.

Add remaining 3 ingredients. Process until combined. Store in airtight container in refrigerator for up to 5 days or in freezer for up to 6 months. Makes about 4 cups (1 L).

*1 cup (250 mL): 175 Calories; 6.4 g Total Fat (1.2 g Mono, 0.8 g Poly, 3.9 g Sat); 11 mg Cholesterol; 25 g Carbohydrate; 8 g Fibre; 9 g Protein; 390 mg Sodium*

Pictured on page 125.

# Cilantro Tomato Sauce

*Sure, some pasta sauces are better if you let them simmer all day, but this one's quick as a wink! It's filled with the fresh, bright flavours of tomato and cilantro that are better without long cooking. Serve over long pastas.*

| | | |
|---|---|---|
| Olive (or cooking) oil | 1 tbsp. | 15 mL |
| Chopped onion | 1 cup | 250 mL |
| Garlic cloves, minced | 2 | 2 |
| (or 1/2 tsp., 2 mL, powder) | | |
| Can of diced tomatoes (with juice) | 28 oz. | 796 mL |
| Granulated sugar | 1 tsp. | 5 mL |
| Salt | 1/2 tsp. | 2 mL |
| Chopped fresh cilantro | 1/2 cup | 125 mL |

Heat olive oil in large saucepan on medium. Add onion and garlic. Cook, uncovered, for 5 to 10 minutes, stirring often, until onion is softened.

Add next 3 ingredients. Stir. Simmer for about 5 minutes to blend flavours. Remove from heat.

Add cilantro. Stir. Store in airtight container in refrigerator for up to 3 days or freezer for up to 1 month. Makes about 3 1/2 cups (875 mL).

*1 cup (250 mL): 99 Calories; 4.1 g Total Fat (2.9 g Mono, 0.6 g Poly, 0.6 g Sat); 0 mg Cholesterol; 16 g Carbohydrate; 1 g Fibre; 2 g Protein; 953 mg Sodium*

# Slow Cooker Mushroom Sauce

*Easy to make and delightful to enjoy—especially considering your slow cooker will do most of the work.*

| | | |
|---|---|---|
| Butter (or hard margarine) | 1 tbsp. | 15 mL |
| Sliced fresh white mushrooms | 3 cups | 750 mL |
| Chopped onion | 1 cup | 250 mL |
| Dried thyme | 1 tsp. | 5 mL |
| Cans of condensed cream of mushroom soup (10 oz., 284 mL, each) | 2 | 2 |
| Water | 1 cup | 250 mL |
| Half-and-half cream | 1 cup | 250 mL |

*(continued on next page)*

**130**

Sauces

Heat butter in large frying pan on medium-high until melted. Add next 3 ingredients. Cook for 5 to 10 minutes, stirring occasionally, until onion is softened. Transfer vegetables and any liquid to 3 1/2 to 4 quart (3.5 to 4 L) slow cooker.

Combine soup and water in small bowl. Add to slow cooker. Stir. Cook, covered, on Low for 4 to 6 hours or on High for 2 to 3 hours.

Add cream. Stir. Cook, covered, on High for 15 minutes until heated through. Store in airtight container in refrigerator for up to 3 days or in freezer for up to 1 month. Makes about 4 cups (1 L).

*1/2 cup (125 mL): 124 Calories; 9.0 g Total Fat (1.4 g Mono, 0.2 g Poly, 3.9 g Sat); 18 mg Cholesterol; 9 g Carbohydrate; 1 g Fibre; 2 g Protein; 530 mg Sodium*

# Parma Sauce

*Just about the most versatile sauce you could find—the possibilities are endless! Try adding cooked meat, seafood or veggies. Or, for a richer sauce, substitute half-and-half cream for the milk or add a garnish of grated Parmesan.*

| Butter (or hard margarine) | 2 tbsp. | 30 mL |
| All-purpose flour | 2 tbsp. | 30 mL |
| Milk | 2 cups | 500 mL |
| Salt | 1/4 tsp. | 1 mL |
| Pepper | 1/8 tsp. | 0.5 mL |
| Grated Parmesan cheese | 2/3 cup | 150 mL |

Melt butter in medium saucepan on medium. Add flour. Heat and stir for 1 minute.

Slowly add next 3 ingredients, stirring constantly, until smooth. Heat and stir for 5 to 10 minutes until boiling and thickened. Remove from heat.

Add cheese. Stir until melted. Makes about 2 cups (500 mL).

*1/2 cup (125 mL): 198 Calories; 12.9 g Total Fat (2.0 g Mono, 0.2 g Poly, 8.3 g Sat); 43 mg Cholesterol; 9 g Carbohydrate; trace Fibre; 13 g Protein; 590 mg Sodium*

Pictured on page 126.

**PARMA ROSA SAUCE:** Stir in 2 tbsp. (30 mL) tomato paste before adding cheese.

Pictured on page 17.

**PARMA PESTO SAUCE:** Stir in 1 tbsp. (15 mL) basil pesto before adding cheese.

# Family Meat Sauce

*Finally, a sauce the whole family will love! A big batch of this beefy sauce is easily made in your slow cooker and can be frozen for speedy weeknight meals or layered in Family Lasagna, page 40.*

| | | |
|---|---|---|
| Cooking oil | 2 tsp. | 10 mL |
| Lean ground beef | 2 lbs. | 900 g |
| Cooking oil | 1 tsp. | 5 mL |
| Chopped onion | 2 cups | 500 mL |
| Garlic cloves, minced | 2 | 2 |
| (or 1/2 tsp., 2 mL, powder) | | |
| Sliced fresh white mushrooms | 4 cups | 1 L |
| Chopped green pepper | 2 cups | 500 mL |
| Italian seasoning | 1 tbsp. | 15 mL |
| Can of diced tomatoes (with juice) | 28 oz. | 796 mL |
| Tomato pasta sauce | 3 cups | 750 mL |
| Salt | 3/4 tsp. | 4 mL |
| Bay leaves | 2 | 2 |

Heat first amount of cooking oil in large frying pan on medium. Add beef. Scramble-fry for about 10 minutes until no longer pink. Transfer to 5 to 6 quart (5 to 6 L) slow cooker.

Heat second amount of cooking oil in same frying pan on medium. Add onion and garlic. Cook for about 5 minutes, stirring often, until onion is softened.

Add next 3 ingredients. Cook for about 10 minutes until softened. Add to beef. Stir.

Add remaining 4 ingredients. Stir well. Transfer to slow cooker. Cook, covered, on Low for 10 to 12 hours or on High for 5 to 6 hours. Remove and discard bay leaves. Store in airtight container in refrigerator for up to 5 days or in freezer for up to 6 months. Makes about 12 cups (3 L).

*1 cup (250 mL): 206 Calories; 9.3 g Total Fat (4.0 g Mono, 0.6 g Poly, 3.2 g Sat); 49 mg Cholesterol; 13 g Carbohydrate; 2 g Fibre; 18 g Protein; 665 mg Sodium*

# Meaty Spaghetti Sauce

*Really hungry? A big helping of spaghetti with this rich and hearty meat
sauce definitely fits the bill. This sauce also works great for lasagna. If you
like it really spicy, add more hot sauce and chilies.*

| | | |
|---|---|---|
| Olive (or cooking) oil | 1 tsp. | 5 mL |
| Lean ground beef | 1 lb. | 454 g |
| Chopped onion | 1 cup | 250 mL |
| Garlic cloves, minced | 4 | 4 |
| (or 1 tsp., 5 mL, powder) | | |
| Can of crushed tomatoes | 28 oz. | 796 mL |
| Can of diced tomatoes (with juice) | 28 oz. | 796 mL |
| Parsley flakes | 2 tbsp. | 30 mL |
| Dried oregano | 1 tbsp. | 15 mL |
| Granulated sugar | 1 tbsp. | 15 mL |
| Worcestershire sauce | 1 tbsp. | 15 mL |
| Dried basil | 2 tsp. | 10 mL |
| Hot pepper sauce | 1/2 tsp. | 2 mL |
| Salt | 1/2 tsp. | 2 mL |
| Pepper | 1/2 tsp. | 2 mL |
| Celery seed | 1/4 tsp. | 1 mL |
| Dried crushed chilies | 1/4 tsp. | 1 mL |

Heat olive oil in large saucepan on medium. Add next 3 ingredients.
Scramble-fry for about 10 minutes until beef is no longer pink.

Add remaining 12 ingredients. Stir. Bring to a boil. Reduce heat to
medium-low. Simmer, partially covered, for 30 minutes to blend flavours.
Store in airtight container in refrigerator for up to 5 days or in freezer for
up to 6 months. Makes about 8 1/2 cups (2.1 L).

*1 cup (250 mL): 166 Calories; 6.0 g Total Fat (2.7 g Mono, 0.3 g Poly, 2.3 g Sat); 35 mg Cholesterol;
15 g Carbohydrate; 2 g Fibre; 13 g Protein; 603 mg Sodium*

# Classic Pesto Sauce

*Infinite possibilities in a sauce that packs some serious flavour punch! It's wonderful on gnocchi or other noodles, but you can also try it with mashed potatoes, steamed vegetables, grilled meats, or whatever else you can imagine.*

| | | |
|---|---|---|
| Fresh basil leaves, packed | 2 cups | 500 mL |
| Olive oil | 1/4 cup | 60 mL |
| Pine nuts, toasted (see Tip, page 104) | 1/4 cup | 60 mL |
| Garlic cloves | 3 | 3 |
| Salt | 1/4 tsp. | 1 mL |
| Grated Parmesan cheese | 1/2 cup | 125 mL |

Process first 5 ingredients in blender until smooth. Transfer to small bowl.

Add cheese. Stir well. Store in refrigerator for up to 3 days (see Note). Makes about 1 cup (250 mL).

*1/4 cup (60 mL): 235 Calories; 23.3 g Total Fat (11.1 g Mono, 4.8 g Poly, 5.2 g Sat); 14 g Cholesterol; 3 g Carbohydrate; 1 g Fibre; 7 g Protein; 383 mg Sodium*

**Note:** To store, put into airtight container. Place a piece of plastic wrap directly on top of pesto. Cover with lid.

**PARSLEY PESTO SAUCE:** Use same amount of parsley instead of basil.

# Walnut Gorgonzola Sauce

*If you're not overly fond of blue cheese, this rich and flavourful sauce will have you rethinking your preferences. Mild Gorgonzola pairs perfectly with crunchy walnuts. Serve it over your favourite pasta.*

| | | |
|---|---|---|
| Butter (or hard margarine) | 2 tbsp. | 30 mL |
| Finely chopped walnuts | 1/2 cup | 125 mL |
| All-purpose flour | 1/4 cup | 60 mL |
| Milk | 3 cups | 750 mL |
| Ground nutmeg | 1/8 tsp. | 0.5 mL |
| Gorgonzola cheese | 5 oz. | 140 g |
| Salt | 1/4 tsp. | 1 mL |

*(continued on next page)*

Melt butter in large saucepan on medium-low. Add walnuts. Cook, uncovered, for about 15 minutes, stirring often, until golden.

Sprinkle with flour. Heat and stir for 1 minute. Increase heat to medium. Slowly add milk and nutmeg, stirring constantly, until smooth. Heat and stir on medium for about 5 minutes until boiling and thickened.

Add cheese and salt. Remove from heat. Stir until smooth. Store in airtight container in refrigerator for up to 3 days. Makes about 4 cups (1 L).

*1/2 cup (125 mL): 191 Calories; 14.3 g Total Fat (1.8 g Mono, 3.6 g Poly, 6.6 g Sat); 29 mg Cholesterol; 9 g Carbohydrate; 1 g Fibre; 9 g Protein; 385 mg Sodium*

---

# Green Pepper Sausage Sauce

*The hearty flavours of pepper and Italian sausage in a tomato sauce are a fabulous fit for rotini or radiatore pasta.*

| | | |
|---|---|---|
| Cooking oil | 1/2 tsp. | 2 mL |
| Italian sausage, casing removed | 3/4 lb. | 340 g |
| Can of diced tomatoes (with juice) | 28 oz. | 796 mL |
| Chopped green pepper | 2 cups | 500 mL |
| Chopped onion | 1 cup | 250 mL |
| Dried basil | 1 tsp. | 5 mL |
| Dried oregano | 1 tsp. | 5 mL |

Heat cooking oil in large frying pan on medium. Add sausage. Scramble-fry for 5 to 10 minutes until no longer pink. Drain.

Add remaining 5 ingredients. Stir. Bring to a boil. Reduce heat to medium-low. Simmer for about 30 minutes, stirring occasionally, until thickened and vegetables are tender. Store in airtight container for up to 5 days or in freezer for up to 3 months. Makes about 6 cups (1.5 L).

*1 cup (250 mL): 147 Calories; 8.4 g Total Fat (3.7 g Mono, 1.1 g Poly, 2.8 g Sat); 16 mg Cholesterol; 12 g Carbohydrate; 1 g Fibre; 7 g Protein; 712 mg Sodium*

Pictured on page 125.

# Mushroom Thyme Sauce

*It's thyme you tried something different. Earthy mushrooms, beef broth and a touch of sherry result in a full-flavoured sauce that compliments any type of pasta and is particularly good on gnocchi.*

| | | |
|---|---|---|
| Package of dried shiitake mushrooms | 3/4 oz. | 22 g |
| Hot prepared beef broth | 1 cup | 250 mL |
| Butter (or hard margarine) | 2 tbsp. | 30 mL |
| Finely chopped onion | 1/3 cup | 75 mL |
| Thinly sliced fresh brown (or white) mushrooms | 4 cups | 1 L |
| Half-and-half cream | 1/2 cup | 125 mL |
| Dry sherry | 2 tbsp. | 30 mL |
| Chopped fresh thyme (or 1/4 tsp., 1 mL, dried) | 1 tsp. | 5 mL |
| Salt | 1/4 tsp. | 1 mL |
| Pepper | 1/4 tsp. | 1 mL |

Put dried mushrooms into small heatproof bowl. Add hot broth. Stir. Let stand, covered, for about 15 minutes until softened. Remove mushrooms with slotted spoon. Strain broth through a triple layer of cheesecloth into separate small bowl. Set aside. Thinly slice mushrooms, discarding stems if tough.

Melt butter in large frying pan on medium. Add onion, fresh and dried mushrooms. Cook for about 10 minutes, stirring occasionally, until mushrooms start to brown.

Add cream, sherry and reserved broth. Bring to a boil. Reduce heat to medium-low. Simmer for about 10 minutes until sauce has thickened.

Add remaining 3 ingredients. Heat and stir for 1 minute until fragrant. Makes about 1 3/4 cups (425 mL).

*1/2 cup (125 mL): 156 Calories; 10.8 g Total Fat (2.9 g Mono, 0.5 g Poly, 6.7 g Sat); 30 mg Cholesterol; 12 g Carbohydrate; 1 g Fibre; 4 g Protein; 622 mg Sodium*

# Smoked Salmon Sauce

*Luxurious smoked salmon lends its rich flavour to this light and luscious sauce. Serve over angel hair pasta for a sure-fire hit with any seafood lover.*

| | | |
|---|---|---|
| Butter (or hard margarine) | 1 tbsp. | 15 mL |
| Finely chopped green onion | 3 tbsp. | 50 mL |
| Can of 2% evaporated milk | 13 1/2 oz. | 385 mL |
| Dry (or alcohol-free) white wine | 1/3 cup | 75 mL |
| Prepared chicken broth | 1/2 cup | 125 mL |
| Cornstarch | 2 tsp. | 10 mL |
| Smoked salmon, cut into thin strips | 4 oz. | 113 g |
| Chopped fresh dill | 1 tbsp. | 15 mL |
| Lemon juice | 1 tsp. | 5 mL |

Heat butter in large frying pan on medium. Add green onion. Cook for about 3 minutes, stirring occasionally, until softened.

Add milk and wine. Stir. Bring to a boil. Boil gently for 5 minutes.

Stir broth into cornstarch in small cup. Add to wine mixture. Heat and stir for about 1 minute until boiling and thickened.

Add remaining 3 ingredients. Heat and stir for about 2 minutes until salmon is heated through. Serve immediately. Makes about 2 1/2 cups (625 mL).

*1/2 cup (125 mL): 137 Calories; 4.9 g Total Fat (1.5 g Mono, 0.4 g Poly, 2.6 g Sat); 17 mg Cholesterol; 10 g Carbohydrate; trace Fibre; 10 g Protein; 430 mg Sodium*

Pictured on page 125.

## Paré Pointer

*Tough chickens come from hard-boiled eggs.*

# Sweet Potato And Kale Penne

*A most marvelous medley of flavours in this mix of kale, sweet potato, tangy lemon and a hint of ginger. Serve with chicken or fish.*

| | | |
|---|---|---|
| Water | 8 cups | 2 L |
| Salt | 1 tsp. | 5 mL |
| Penne pasta | 1 1/2 cups | 375 mL |
| Cooking oil | 2 tsp. | 10 mL |
| Chopped onion | 1 cup | 250 mL |
| Fresh, peeled yellow-fleshed sweet potatoes, diced | 1 lb. | 454 g |
| Garlic cloves, minced (or 1/2 tsp., 2 mL, powder) | 2 | 2 |
| Finely grated gingerroot | 2 tsp. | 10 mL |
| Prepared vegetable broth | 1 1/2 cups | 375 mL |
| Salt | 1/4 tsp. | 1 mL |
| Pepper | 1/4 tsp. | 1 mL |
| Chopped kale leaves, lightly packed (see Tip, page 99) | 2 cups | 500 mL |
| Lemon juice | 1 tbsp. | 15 mL |
| Grated lemon zest | 1 tsp. | 5 mL |

Combine water and salt in large saucepan. Bring to a boil. Add pasta. Boil, uncovered, for 14 to 16 minutes, stirring occasionally, until tender but firm. Drain. Return to same pot. Cover to keep warm.

Heat cooking oil in large frying pan on medium. Add onion. Cook for 5 to 10 minutes, stirring occasionally, until onion is softened.

Add next 3 ingredients. Heat and stir for 1 minute. Add next 3 ingredients. Bring to a boil. Reduce heat to medium-low. Cook, covered, for 8 to 10 minutes until sweet potato is almost tender.

Add kale. Stir. Cook for 5 to 8 minutes until vegetables are tender. Add to pasta. Toss.

Add lemon juice and zest. Toss. Makes about 7 cups (1.75 L).

*1 cup (250 mL): 177 Calories; 2.1 g Total Fat (0.8 g Mono, 0.5 g Poly, 0.2 g Sat); 0 mg Cholesterol; 35 g Carbohydrate; 4 g Fibre; 5 g Protein; 209 mg Sodium*

Pictured on page 144 and on back cover.

# Peppery Zucchini And Bacon

*Looking for a flavourful side? Smoky bacon, pepper, lemon and cheese add loads of flavour to mild-tasting zucchini. Serve it up with a main course of chicken, pork or fish.*

| | | |
|---|---|---|
| Water | 8 cups | 2 L |
| Salt | 1 tsp. | 5 mL |
| Rigatoni pasta | 3 cups | 750 mL |
| Bacon slices, chopped | 4 | 4 |
| Sliced zucchini (with peel), halved lengthwise and sliced crosswise into 1/4 inch (6 mm) pieces | 2 cups | 500 mL |
| Chopped onion | 1/2 cup | 125 mL |
| Garlic cloves, minced (or 1/2 tsp., 2 mL, powder) | 2 | 2 |
| Grated Greek Myzithra (or Parmesan) cheese | 1/4 cup | 60 mL |
| Lemon juice | 2 tbsp. | 30 mL |
| Coarsely ground pepper | 1/2 tsp. | 2 mL |
| Grated lemon zest | 1/2 tsp. | 2 mL |

Combine water and salt in large saucepan. Bring to a boil. Add pasta. Boil, uncovered, for 14 to 16 minutes, stirring occasionally, until tender but firm. Drain. Return to same pot. Cover to keep warm.

Cook bacon in large frying pan on medium until crisp. Remove with slotted spoon to paper towel-lined plate to drain. Drain and discard all but 1 tbsp. (15 mL) drippings.

Add next 3 ingredients. Cook for about 5 minutes, stirring occasionally, until zucchini is tender-crisp. Remove from heat. Add bacon. Stir.

Add remaining 4 ingredients and zucchini mixture to pasta. Toss. Makes about 6 cups (1.5 L).

*1 cup (250 mL): 190 Calories; 5.8 g Total Fat (1.8 g Mono, 0.5 g Poly, 2.4 g Sat); 13 mg Cholesterol; 26 g Carbohydrate; 2 g Fibre; 9 g Protein; 499 mg Sodium*

Pictured on page 143.

# Roasted Vegetable Farfalle

*Tender, roasted vegetables with farfalle (pronounced fahr-FAH-lay), also known as bow tie pasta, dressed in a sweet and tangy vinaigrette. Serve with grilled meats for a complete meal.*

| | | |
|---|---|---|
| Chopped zucchini (with peel), 1/2 inch (12 mm) pieces | 2 cups | 500 mL |
| Halved fresh white mushrooms | 2 cups | 500 mL |
| Chopped onion (1 inch, 2.5 cm, pieces) | 1 cup | 250 mL |
| Chopped red pepper (1 inch, 2.5 cm, pieces) | 1 cup | 250 mL |
| Cooking oil | 3 tbsp. | 50 mL |
| Salt | 1/2 tsp. | 2 mL |
| Pepper | 1/4 tsp. | 1 mL |
| Water | 8 cups | 2 L |
| Salt | 1 tsp. | 5 mL |
| Medium bow pasta | 2 cups | 500 mL |
| Rice vinegar | 2 tbsp. | 30 mL |
| Maple (or maple-flavoured) syrup | 1 tbsp. | 15 mL |
| Sesame oil (for flavour) | 2 tsp. | 10 mL |
| Soy sauce | 2 tsp. | 10 mL |
| Ground ginger | 1 tsp. | 5 mL |
| Pepper | 1/4 tsp. | 1 mL |

Put first 7 ingredients into large bowl. Toss until coated. Spread on greased large baking sheet with sides. Bake in 400°F (205°C) oven for about 25 minutes until tender.

Combine water and salt in large saucepan. Bring to a boil. Add pasta. Boil, uncovered, for 10 to 12 minutes, stirring occasionally, until tender but firm. Drain. Return to same pot.

Combine remaining 6 ingredients in small bowl. Add to pasta. Toss. Add roasted vegetables. Toss gently. Makes about 5 cups (1.25 L).

*1 cup (250 mL): 190 Calories; 10.9 g Total Fat (4.9 g Mono, 2.8 g Poly, 1.0 g Sat); 0 mg Cholesterol; 22 g Carbohydrate; 2 g Fibre; 4 g Protein; 419 mg Sodium*

Pictured on page 143.

# Rotini Pepper Medley

*Has there ever been a more colourful dish? With four colours of peppers in a rich cream sauce, your eyes will enjoy this dish just as much as your taste buds. Try substituting coloured rotini for an even more colourful side.*

| | | |
|---|---|---|
| Water | 8 cups | 2 L |
| Salt | 1 tsp. | 5 mL |
| Rotini pasta | 2 1/2 cups | 625 mL |
| Butter (or hard margarine) | 1 tbsp. | 30 mL |
| Thinly sliced green pepper | 1/2 cup | 125 mL |
| Thinly sliced onion | 1/2 cup | 125 mL |
| Thinly sliced orange pepper | 1/2 cup | 125 mL |
| Thinly sliced red pepper | 1/2 cup | 125 mL |
| Thinly sliced yellow pepper | 1/2 cup | 125 mL |
| Garlic cloves, minced | 2 | 2 |
| (or 1/2 tsp., 2 mL, powder) | | |
| Prepared chicken broth | 2 cups | 500 mL |
| All-purpose flour | 2 tbsp. | 30 mL |
| Greek seasoning | 1 tsp. | 5 mL |
| Cream cheese, cubed | 2 oz. | 57 g |
| Crumbled feta cheese | 2 oz. | 57 g |

Combine water and salt in large saucepan. Bring to a boil. Add pasta. Boil, uncovered, for 12 to 14 minutes, stirring occasionally, until tender but firm. Drain. Return to same pot. Cover to keep warm.

Melt butter in large frying pan on medium. Add next 6 ingredients. Cook for 5 to 10 minutes, stirring occasionally, until onion is softened. Add to pasta. Toss. Cover to keep warm.

Add 1 cup (250 mL) broth to same frying pan. Bring to a boil on medium. Whisk flour, Greek seasoning and remaining broth in small bowl until smooth. Add to pan. Heat and stir for 1 to 2 minutes until boiling and thickened.

Add cream cheese and feta cheese. Stir until melted. Add to pasta mixture. Stir to coat. Makes about 4 1/2 cups (1.1 L).

*1 cup (250 mL): 287 Calories; 11.0 g Total Fat (1.4 g Mono, 0.4 g Poly, 6.3 g Sat); 31 mg Cholesterol; 38 g Carbohydrate; 3 g Fibre; 9 g Protein; 860 mg Sodium*

# Greek Cheese And Butter Spaghetti

*Hard, salty Myzithra (pronounced mih-ZEE-thra) cheese and fresh herbs are tossed in browned butter for a simple, yet impressive side. The cheese should be available at your deli counter, but you can substitute Romano or Greek Kefalotyri cheese instead.*

| | | |
|---|---|---|
| Water | 12 cups | 3 L |
| Salt | 1 1/2 tsp. | 7 mL |
| Spaghetti | 8 oz. | 225 g |
| Butter | 1/3 cup | 75 mL |
| Garlic clove, minced | 1 | 1 |
| (or 1/4 tsp., 1 mL, powder) | | |
| Grated Greek Myzithra cheese | 3/4 cup | 175 mL |
| Chopped fresh basil | 1 tbsp. | 15 mL |
| Chopped fresh oregano | 1 tbsp. | 15 mL |

Combine water and salt in Dutch oven. Bring to a boil. Add pasta. Boil, uncovered, for 10 to 12 minutes, stirring occasionally, until tender but firm. Drain. Return to same pot. Cover to keep warm.

Heat butter in small frying pan on medium until foamy and starting to turn golden. Add garlic. Heat and stir for about 2 minutes until butter browns. Add to pasta.

Add remaining 3 ingredients. Toss. Serve immediately. Makes about 4 cups (1 L).

*1 cup (250 mL): 442 Calories; 20.8 g Total Fat (3.9 g Mono, 0.6 g Poly, 13.0 g Sat); 63 mg Cholesterol; 45 g Carbohydrate; 2 g Fibre; 18 g Protein; 1545 mg Sodium*

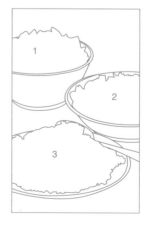

1. Peppery Zucchini And Bacon, page 139
2. Roasted Vegetable Farfalle, page 140
3. Bacon And Pea Fusilli, page 147

Props courtesy of: Out of the Fire Studio
Island Pottery Inc.

# Aniseed Tomato Fusilli

*A hint of licorice flavour balances the saltiness of olives and feta in this simple pasta side. Try it with grilled chicken breast or pork.*

| | | |
|---|---|---|
| Water | 8 cups | 2 L |
| Salt | 1 tsp. | 5 mL |
| Fusilli pasta | 1 1/3 cups | 325 mL |
| Olive (or cooking) oil | 1 tsp. | 5 mL |
| Chopped onion | 1/4 cup | 60 mL |
| Aniseed | 1 tsp. | 5 mL |
| Can of diced tomatoes (with juice) | 14 oz. | 398 mL |
| Dried basil | 1/2 tsp. | 2 mL |
| Chopped pitted kalamata olives | 1/4 cup | 60 mL |
| Crumbled feta cheese | 1/2 cup | 125 mL |

Combine water and salt in large saucepan. Bring to a boil. Add pasta. Boil, uncovered, for 7 to 9 minutes until tender but firm. Drain, reserving 1/3 cup (75 mL) cooking water. Return pasta to same pot. Cover to keep warm.

Heat olive oil in large frying pan on medium. Add onion and aniseed. Cook for about 5 minutes, stirring often, until onion is softened.

Add tomatoes with juice and basil. Bring to a boil. Boil gently for about 5 minutes, stirring occasionally, until slightly reduced.

Add olives. Heat and stir for 1 minute. Add to pasta with reserved cooking water. Stir.

Sprinkle with cheese. Makes about 4 cups (1 L).

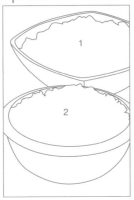

*1 cup (250 mL): 172 Calories; 6.5 g Total Fat (2.4 g Mono, 0.4 g Poly, 3.1 g Sat); 17 mg Cholesterol; 23 g Carbohydrate; 1 g Fibre; 7 g Protein; 554 mg Sodium*

Pictured at left and on back cover.

1. Sweet Potato And Kale Penne, page 138
2. Aniseed Tomato Fusilli, above

Props courtesy of: Cherison Enterprises Inc.

# Lemon Pepper Linguine

*Does the main course require all your attention? This delicious side is so easy that you'll have lots of time to devote to preparing the main attraction.*

| | | |
|---|---|---|
| Water | 12 cups | 3 L |
| Salt | 1 1/2 tsp. | 7 mL |
| Linguine | 8 oz. | 225 g |
| Olive oil | 2 tbsp. | 30 mL |
| Grated lemon zest (see Tip, page 81) | 2 tsp. | 10 mL |
| Lemon juice | 2 tsp. | 10 mL |
| Salt | 1/4 tsp. | 1 mL |
| Coarsely ground pepper | 2 tsp. | 10 mL |

Combine water and salt in Dutch oven. Bring to a boil. Add pasta. Boil, uncovered, for 9 to 11 minutes, stirring occasionally, until tender but firm. Drain. Return to same pot.

Add remaining 5 ingredients. Toss. Makes about 3 1/2 cups (875 mL).

*1 cup (250 mL): 318 Calories; 9.2 g Total Fat (5.7 g Mono, 1.1 g Poly, 1.1 g Sat); 0 mg Cholesterol; 50 g Carbohydrate; 3 g Fibre; 9 g Protein; 166 mg Sodium*

# Lemon Pesto Corkscrews

*This recipe features a super-easy homemade pesto with the fresh flavours of basil, lemon and pine nuts. Attractive and easy—this side is delicious with chicken or pork.*

| | | |
|---|---|---|
| Water | 8 cups | 2 L |
| Salt | 1 tsp. | 5 mL |
| Cavatappi pasta | 3 cups | 750 mL |
| Fresh basil leaves, packed | 1 cup | 250 mL |
| Lemon juice | 2 tbsp. | 30 mL |
| Pine nuts, toasted (see Tip, page 104) | 2 tbsp. | 30 mL |
| Olive (or cooking) oil | 2 tsp. | 10 mL |
| Garlic cloves | 1 | 1 |
| Grated Parmesan cheese | 1/2 cup | 125 mL |
| Salt | 1/8 tsp. | 0.5 mL |

*(continued on next page)*

Combine water and salt in large saucepan. Bring to a boil. Add pasta. Boil, uncovered, for 10 to 12 minutes, stirring occasionally, until tender but firm. Drain, reserving 1/2 cup (125 mL) cooking water. Return pasta to same pot. Cover to keep warm.

Meanwhile, process next 5 ingredients in blender or food processor until smooth. Transfer to small bowl.

Add cheese and salt. Stir. Add to pasta with reserved cooking water. Stir to coat. Makes about 4 1/2 cups (1.1 L).

*1 cup (250 mL):* 318 Calories; 10.0 g Total Fat (2.4 g Mono, 2.1 g Poly, 3.4 g Sat); 13 mg Cholesterol; 44 g Carbohydrate; 3 g Fibre; 14 g Protein; 293 mg Sodium

# Bacon And Pea Fusilli

*A little bacon goes a long way when it's tossed with fresh-tasting green peas, leeks and lemon. Serve up this sensational side with a saucy main course.*

| | | |
|---|---|---|
| Water | 8 cups | 2 L |
| Salt | 1 tsp. | 5 mL |
| Fusilli pasta | 1 1/2 cups | 375 mL |
| Bacon slices, chopped | 4 | 4 |
| Thinly sliced leek (white part only) | 1 cup | 250 mL |
| Garlic clove, minced | 1 | 1 |
| (or 1/4 tsp., 1 mL, powder) | | |
| Frozen peas | 1 cup | 250 mL |
| Grated lemon zest | 1 tsp. | 5 mL |

Combine water and salt in large saucepan. Bring to a boil. Add pasta. Boil, uncovered, for 7 to 9 minutes, stirring occasionally, until tender but firm. Drain, reserving 1/4 cup (60 mL) cooking water. Return to same pot. Cover to keep warm.

Combine next 3 ingredients in large frying pan on medium. Cook, stirring occasionally, until leek is softened. Add peas and reserved cooking water. Stir. Bring to a boil. Simmer for about 2 minutes until peas are tender. Add pasta. Toss.

Sprinkle with lemon zest. Toss. Makes about 4 cups (1 L).

*1 cup (250 mL):* 245 Calories; 10.9 g Total Fat (4.6 g Mono, 1.2 g Poly, 3.5 g Sat); 15 mg Cholesterol; 28 g Carbohydrate; 4 g Fibre; 9 g Protein; 256 mg Sodium

Pictured on page 143.

Sides

# Saucy Fettuccine

*A rich and creamy pasta side—with a simple three-ingredient sauce! Just as easy as preparing a packaged pasta side, but with far better results.*

| | | |
|---|---|---|
| Water | 12 cups | 3 L |
| Salt | 1 1/2 tsp. | 7 mL |
| Fettuccine | 8 oz. | 225 g |
| Herb and garlic cream cheese, softened | 4 oz. | 113 g |
| 2% cottage cheese | 1/2 cup | 125 mL |
| Chopped fresh parsley | 1 tbsp. | 15 mL |

Combine water and salt in Dutch oven. Bring to a boil. Add pasta. Boil, uncovered, for 11 to 13 minutes, stirring occasionally, until tender but firm. Drain, reserving 1/3 cup (75 mL) cooking water. Return to same pot. Cover to keep warm.

Combine cream cheese and cottage cheese in small saucepan on medium. Add reserved cooking water. Heat and stir until cream cheese is melted. Add to pasta. Toss.

Sprinkle with parsley. Makes about 4 cups (1 L).

*1 cup (250 mL): 329 Calories; 10.6 g Total Fat (0.2 g Mono, trace Poly, 6 g Sat); 41 mg Cholesterol; 45 g Carbohydrate; 2 g Fibre; 13 g Protein; 289 mg Sodium*

# Three-Cheese Spaghetti

*A simple, mild-flavoured dish kids will eat—and adults will love!*

| | | |
|---|---|---|
| Water | 12 cups | 3 L |
| Salt | 1 1/2 tsp. | 7 mL |
| Spaghetti | 11 oz. | 310 g |
| Process cheese spread (see Note) | 1/2 cup | 125 mL |
| Grated mozzarella cheese | 6 tbsp. | 100 mL |
| Butter (or hard margarine) | 2 tbsp. | 30 mL |
| Grated Parmesan cheese | 2 tbsp. | 30 mL |
| Milk | 2 tbsp. | 30 mL |

*(continued on next page)*

Combine water and salt in large saucepan. Bring to a boil. Add spaghetti. Boil, uncovered, for 10 to 12 minutes, stirring occasionally, until tender but firm. Drain. Return to same pot.

Add remaining 5 ingredients. Heat and stir on low for about 1 minute until cheese is melted and spaghetti is coated. Makes about 4 1/2 cups (1.1 L).

*1 cup (250 mL): 420 Calories; 14.0 g Total Fat (1.3 g Mono, 0.2 g Poly, 8.1 g Sat); 41 mg Cholesterol; 56 g Carbohydrate; 3 g Fibre; 17 g Protein; 650 mg Sodium*

**Note:** Use 3 torn up slices of processed cheese if you don't have cheese spread.

# Cajun Orzo Bake

*We are firm believers that easy dishes can be just as delicious as fussy ones. Try this bold-flavoured side with chicken, pork or fish and see if you don't agree.*

| | | |
|---|---|---|
| Cooking oil | 1 tsp. | 5 mL |
| Chopped onion | 1 cup | 250 mL |
| Garlic clove, minced | 1 | 1 |
| (or 1/4 tsp., 1 mL, powder) | | |
| Orzo | 1 1/2 cups | 375 mL |
| Cajun seasoning | 2 tsp. | 10 mL |
| Cayenne pepper | 1/8 tsp. | 0.5 mL |
| Prepared vegetable broth | 2 1/2 cups | 625 mL |

Heat cooking oil in medium saucepan on medium. Add onion and garlic. Cook, uncovered, for 5 to 10 minutes, stirring often, until onion is softened.

Add next 3 ingredients. Heat and stir for 1 minute.

Add broth. Stir. Bring to a boil. Transfer to greased 2 quart (2 L) casserole. Bake, covered, in 400°F (205°C) oven for about 30 minutes until pasta is tender and liquid is absorbed. Makes about 4 cups (1 L).

*1 cup (250 mL): 279 Calories; 2.3 g Total Fat (0.7 g Mono, 0.4 g Poly, 0.1 g Sat); 0 mg Cholesterol; 54 g Carbohydrate; 3 g Fibre; 9 g Protein; 559 mg Sodium*

# Measurement Tables

Throughout this book measurements are given in Conventional and Metric measure. To compensate for differences between the two measurements due to rounding, a full metric measure is not always used. The cup used is the standard 8 fluid ounce. Temperature is given in degrees Fahrenheit and Celsius. Baking pan measurements are in inches and centimetres as well as quarts and litres. An exact metric conversion is given below as well as the working equivalent (Metric Standard Measure).

## Spoons

| Conventional Measure | Metric Exact Conversion Millilitre (mL) | Metric Standard Measure Millilitre (mL) |
|---|---|---|
| 1/8 teaspoon (tsp.) | 0.6 mL | 0.5 mL |
| 1/4 teaspoon (tsp.) | 1.2 mL | 1 mL |
| 1/2 teaspoon (tsp.) | 2.4 mL | 2 mL |
| 1 teaspoon (tsp.) | 4.7 mL | 5 mL |
| 2 teaspoons (tsp.) | 9.4 mL | 10 mL |
| 1 tablespoon (tbsp.) | 14.2 mL | 15 mL |

## Cups

| Conventional Measure | Metric Exact Conversion Millilitre (mL) | Metric Standard Measure Millilitre (mL) |
|---|---|---|
| 1/4 cup (4 tbsp.) | 56.8 mL | 60 mL |
| 1/3 cup (5 1/3 tbsp.) | 75.6 mL | 75 mL |
| 1/2 cup (8 tbsp.) | 113.7 mL | 125 mL |
| 2/3 cup (10 2/3 tbsp.) | 151.2 mL | 150 mL |
| 3/4 cup (12 tbsp.) | 170.5 mL | 175 mL |
| 1 cup (16 tbsp.) | 227.3 mL | 250 mL |
| 4 1/2 cups | 1022.9 mL | 1000 mL (1 L) |

## Oven Temperatures

| Fahrenheit (°F) | Celsius (°C) |
|---|---|
| 175° | 80° |
| 200° | 95° |
| 225° | 110° |
| 250° | 120° |
| 275° | 140° |
| 300° | 150° |
| 325° | 160° |
| 350° | 175° |
| 375° | 190° |
| 400° | 205° |
| 425° | 220° |
| 450° | 230° |
| 475° | 240° |
| 500° | 260° |

## Dry Measurements

| Conventional Measure Ounces (oz.) | Metric Exact Conversion Grams (g) | Metric Standard Measure Grams (g) |
|---|---|---|
| 1 oz. | 28.3 g | 28 g |
| 2 oz. | 56.7 g | 57 g |
| 3 oz. | 85.0 g | 85 g |
| 4 oz. | 113.4 g | 125 g |
| 5 oz. | 141.7 g | 140 g |
| 6 oz. | 170.1 g | 170 g |
| 7 oz. | 198.4 g | 200 g |
| 8 oz. | 226.8 g | 250 g |
| 16 oz. | 453.6 g | 500 g |
| 32 oz. | 907.2 g | 1000 g (1 kg) |

## Pans

| Conventional Inches | Metric Centimetres |
|---|---|
| 8x8 inch | 20x20 cm |
| 9x9 inch | 22x22 cm |
| 9x13 inch | 22x33 cm |
| 10x15 inch | 25x38 cm |
| 11x17 inch | 28x43 cm |
| 8x2 inch round | 20x5 cm |
| 9x2 inch round | 22x5 cm |
| 10x4 1/2 inch tube | 25x11 cm |
| 8x4x3 inch loaf | 20x10x7.5 cm |
| 9x5x3 inch loaf | 22x12.5x7.5 cm |

## Casseroles

| CANADA & BRITAIN Standard Size Casserole | Exact Metric Measure | UNITED STATES Standard Size Casserole | Exact Metric Measure |
|---|---|---|---|
| 1 qt. (5 cups) | 1.13 L | 1 qt. (4 cups) | 900 mL |
| 1 1/2 qts. (7 1/2 cups) | 1.69 L | 1 1/2 qts. (6 cups) | 1.35 L |
| 2 qts. (10 cups) | 2.25 L | 2 qts. (8 cups) | 1.8 L |
| 2 1/2 qts. (12 1/2 cups) | 2.81 L | 2 1/2 qts. (10 cups) | 2.25 L |
| 3 qts. (15 cups) | 3.38 L | 3 qts. (12 cups) | 2.7 L |
| 4 qts. (20 cups) | 4.5 L | 4 qts. (16 cups) | 3.6 L |
| 5 qts. (25 cups) | 5.63 L | 5 qts. (20 cups) | 4.5 L |

# Recipe Index

# P

**156**

# Company's Coming cookbooks are available at retail locations throughout Canada!

## EXCLUSIVE mail order offer on next page
Buy any 2 cookbooks—choose a 3rd FREE of equal or lesser value than the lowest price paid.

## Original Series $15.99

| CODE | | CODE | | CODE | |
|------|--|------|--|------|--|
| SQ | 150 Delicious Squares | CCLFC | Low-Fat Cooking | SDL | School Days Lunches |
| CA | Casseroles | SCH | Stews, Chilies & Chowders | PD | Potluck Dishes |
| MU | Muffins & More | FD | Fondues | GBR | Ground Beef Recipes |
| SA | Salads | CCBE | The Beef Book | FRIR | 4-Ingredient Recipes |
| AP | Appetizers | RC | The Rookie Cook | KHC | Kids' Healthy Cooking |
| CO | Cookies | RHR | Rush-Hour Recipes | MM | Mostly Muffins |
| PA | Pasta | SW | Sweet Cravings | SP | Soups |
| BA | Barbecues | YRG | Year-Round Grilling | SU | Simple Suppers |
| PR | Preserves | GG | Garden Greens | CCDC | Diabetic Cooking |
| CH | Chicken, Etc. | CHC | Chinese Cooking | CHN | Chicken Now |
| CT | Cooking For Two | RL | Recipes For Leftovers | KDS | Kids Do Snacks |
| SC | Slow Cooker Recipes | BEV | The Beverage Book | TMRC | 30-Minute Rookie Cook |
| SF | Stir-Fry | SCD | Slow Cooker Dinners | LFE | Low-Fat Express |
| MAM | Make-Ahead Meals | WM | 30-Minute Weekday Meals | SI | Choosing Sides **NEW** May 1/08 |
| PB | The Potato Book | | | | |

### Cookbook Author Biography

| CODE | $15.99 |
|------|--------|
| JP | Jean Paré: An Appetite for Life |

### Most Loved Recipe Collection

| CODE | $23.99 |
|------|--------|
| MLBQ | Most Loved Barbecuing |
| MLCO | Most Loved Cookies |

| CODE | $24.99 |
|------|--------|
| MLSD | Most Loved Salads & Dressings |
| MLCA | Most Loved Casseroles |
| MLSF | Most Loved Stir-Fries |
| MLHF | Most Loved Holiday Favourites |
| MLSC | Most Loved Slow Cooker Creations |
| MLDE | Most Loved Summertime Desserts **NEW** April 1/08 |

### 3-in-1 Cookbook Collection

| CODE | $29.99 |
|------|--------|
| MNT | Meals in No Time |
| MME | Meals Made Easy **NEW** June 1/08 |

### Lifestyle Series

| CODE | $17.99 |
|------|--------|
| DC | Diabetic Cooking |

| CODE | $19.99 |
|------|--------|
| DDI | Diabetic Dinners |
| HR | Easy Healthy Recipes |
| HH | Healthy in a Hurry |
| WGR | Whole Grain Recipes |

### Special Occasion Series

| CODE | $20.99 |
|------|--------|
| GFK | Gifts from the Kitchen |

| CODE | $24.99 |
|------|--------|
| MLBQ | Christmas Gifts from the Kitchen |
| TR | Timeless Recipes for All Occasions |

| CODE | $27.99 |
|------|--------|
| CCEL | Christmas Celebrations |

| CODE | $29.99 |
|------|--------|
| CATH | Cooking At Home |

# Order ONLINE for fast delivery!

Log onto **www.companyscoming.com**, browse through our library of cookbooks, gift sets and newest releases and place your order using our fast and secure online order form.

## Buy 2, Get 1 FREE!

Buy any 2 cookbooks—choose a **3rd FREE** of equal or lesser value than the lowest price paid.

| Title | Code | Quantity | Price | Total |
|-------|------|----------|-------|-------|
|  |  |  | $ | $ |
|  |  |  |  |  |
|  |  |  |  |  |
|  |  |  |  |  |
|  |  |  |  |  |
|  |  |  |  |  |

DON'T FORGET to indicate your FREE BOOK(S). (see exclusive mail order offer above) PLEASE PRINT

**TOTAL BOOKS** (including FREE)

**TOTAL BOOKS PURCHASED:**

|  | INTERNATIONAL via Air Mail | USA | Canada |
|---|---|---|---|
| **Shipping & Handling First Book** (per destination) | $ 32.98 (one book) | $ 9.98 (one book) | $ 5.98 (one book) |
| Additional Books (include FREE books) | $ ($7.99 each) | $ ($1.99 each) | $ ($1.99 each) |
| **Sub-Total** | $ | $ | $ |
| Canadian residents add GST/HST |  |  | $ |
| **TOTAL AMOUNT ENCLOSED** | $ | $ | $ |

## Terms
- All orders must be prepaid. Sorry, no CODs.
- Canadian orders are processed in Canadian funds, US International orders. are processed in US Funds.
- Prices are subject to change without prior notice.
- Canadian residents must pay GST/HST (no provincial tax required).
- No tax is required for orders outside Canada.
- Satisfaction is guaranteed or return within 30 days for a full refund.
- Make cheque or money order payable to: **Company's Coming Publishing Limited** 2311-96 Street, Edmonton, Alberta Canada T6N 1G3.
- Orders are shipped surface mail. For courier rates, visit our website: **www.companyscoming.com** or contact us: **Tel: 780-450-6223 Fax: 780-450-1857.**

## Gift Giving
- Let us help you with your gift giving!
- We will send cookbooks directly to the recipients of your choice if you give us their names and addresses.
- Please specify the titles you wish to send to each person.
- If you would like to include a personal note or card, we will be pleased to enclose it with your gift order.
- Company's Coming Cookbooks make excellent gifts: birthdays, bridal showers, Mother's Day, Father's Day, graduation or any occasion …collect them all!

☐ MasterCard    ☐ VISA    Expiry _____ / _____ MO/YR

Credit Card # _____

Name of cardholder _____

Cardholder signature _____

## Shipping Address Send the cookbooks listed above to:
☐ **Please check if this is a Gift Order**

Name: _____

Street: _____

City: _____    Prov./State: _____

Postal Code/Zip: _____    Country: _____

Tel: ( _____ ) _____

E-mail address: _____

Your privacy is important to us. We will not share your e-mail address or personal information with any outside party.

☐ **YES! Please add me to your News Bite e-mail newsletter.**

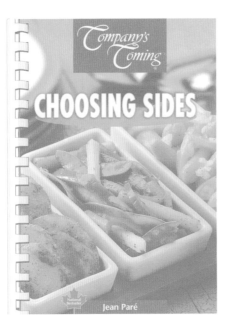

You have your entree picked, now what? With more than 130 quick and easy side dishes, you have options galore for completing your meal. Keep this book close at hand—it's going to be a dinner-planning staple.

Company's Coming
**COOKBOOKS**®

Quick
&
Easy
Recipes

Everyday
Ingredients

Canada's
most popular
cookbooks!